Developing Your Investing Beliefs

What are your investing beliefs? Most investors haven't taken the time to consider that question, let alone to answer it. During the sharp stock market slide in 2008, some investors started following particular gurus who claimed to have predicted the financial crisis. These investors wanted to believe that someone out there could predict important financial events and tell folks how to time their investments to benefit from what was about to unfold. Such market timing is a fool's errand. It sounds possible, and we'd like to believe that it is possible, but it's not possible on the scale various charlatans would have you believe.

As a reader of this book, you probably have a better idea of your investment beliefs than most investors do. To help you along in this process, here are some beliefs for you to consider:

- ✔ **Your own personal comfort matters.** A wide range of investments are available to you, including stocks, exchange-traded funds (ETFs), mutual funds, real estate, and small business. Some folks are simply more comfortable with particular investments, so you shouldn't force yourself into a portfolio that's recommended as being best for you. Consider the value of your time and your investing skills and desires. Investing in stocks and other securities via the best mutual funds and ETFs is both time-efficient and profitable. Real estate investing and running a small business are the most time-intensive investments.

- ✔ **Costs matter.** The more you pay in commissions and management fees on your investments, the greater the drag on your returns. And don't fall prey to thinking that you get what you pay for. Take advantage of tax-deductible retirement accounts, and understand the effect of your tax bracket when investing outside tax-sheltered retirement accounts. Minimize your trading. The more you trade, the more likely you are to make mistakes. Also, you suffer increased transaction costs and higher taxes for non-retirement-account investments.

✔ **Market timing is much harder to predict than folks realize.** Don't bail when things look bleak. The hardest time, psychologically, to hold on to your investments is when they're down. Even the best investments go through depressed periods, which is the worst possible time to sell. Don't sell when there's a sale going on; if anything, consider buying more. Ignore soothsayers and prognosticators. Predicting the future is nearly impossible.

✔ **There are better times than others to sell.** When you're really feeling good about an asset class like stocks, and those assets have had a multiple-year run and are getting widespread accolades, that's a good time to lighten up if you have other good reasons for doing so. By contrast, you can bump up your stock allocation if you're comfortable doing so after a major market decline.

✔ **Think long-term.** Because ownership investments like stocks, real estate, and small business are more volatile, you must keep your long-term perspective when investing in them. Don't invest money in such investments unless you plan to hold them for a minimum of five years and preferably for a decade or longer.

✔ **Diversify.** Diversification is a powerful investment concept that helps you reduce the risk of holding more-aggressive investments. Diversifying simply means that you hold a variety of investments that don't move in tandem in different market environments. When investing in stocks, for example, invest worldwide. You can diversify further by investing in real estate.

✔ **Emphasize value.** Over the long term, value-oriented investments tend to produce higher returns with less volatility than do pure growth-oriented investments.

✔ **Ignore the minutiae.** Don't feel mystified by or feel the need to follow the short-term gyrations of the financial markets. Ultimately, the prices of stocks, bonds, and other financial instruments are determined by supply and demand, which are influenced by thousands of external issues, including millions of investors' expectations and fears.

✔ **You are what you read and listen to.** Don't pollute your mind with bad investing strategies and philosophies. The quality of what you read and listen to is far more important than the quantity.

Praise for Eric Tyson

"Eric Tyson For President!!! Thanks for such a wonderful guide. With a clear, no-nonsense approach to . . . investing for the long haul, Tyson's book says it all without being the least bit long-winded. Pick up a copy today. It'll be your wisest investment ever!!!"

— Jim Beggs, VA

"Eric Tyson is doing something important — namely, helping people at all income levels to take control of their financial futures. This book is a natural outgrowth of Tyson's vision that he has nurtured for years. Like Henry Ford, he wants to make something that was previously accessible only to the wealthy accessible to middle-income Americans."

— James C. Collins, coauthor of the national bestsellers *Built to Last* and *Good to Great*

"Among my favorite financial guides are . . . Eric Tyson's *Personal Finance For Dummies.*"

— Jonathan Clements, *The Wall Street Journal*

"In *Investing For Dummies,* Tyson handily dispatches both the basics . . . and the more complicated."

— Lisa M. Sodders, *The Capital-Journal*

"Smart advice for dummies . . . skip the tomes . . . and buy *Personal Finance For Dummies,* which rewards your candor with advice and comfort."

— Temma Ehrenfeld, *Newsweek*

"Eric Tyson . . . seems the perfect writer for a *...For Dummies* book. He doesn't tell you what to do or consider doing without explaining the why's and how's — and the booby traps to avoid — in plain English. . . . It will lead you through the thickets of your own finances as painlessly as I can imagine."

— Clarence Peterson, *Chicago Tribune*

"*Personal Finance For Dummies* is the perfect book for people who feel guilty about inadequately managing their money but are intimidated by all of the publications out there. It's a painless way to learn how to take control."

— Karen Tofte, producer, National Public Radio's *Sound Money*

More Best-Selling For Dummies Titles by Eric Tyson

Personal Finance in Your 20s For Dummies®

This hands-on, friendly guide provides you with the targeted financial advice you need to establish firm financial footing in your 20s and to secure your finances for years to come. When it comes to protecting your financial future, starting sooner rather than later is the smartest thing you can do. Also check out *Personal Finance For Dummies*.

Mutual Funds For Dummies®

This best-selling guide is now updated to include current fund and portfolio recommendations. Using the practical tips and techniques, you'll design a mutual fund investment plan suited for your income, lifestyle, and risk preferences.

Home Buying For Dummies®

America's No. 1 real estate book includes coverage of online resources in addition to sound financial advice from Eric Tyson and front-line real estate insights from industry veteran Ray Brown. Also available from America's best-selling real estate team of Tyson and Brown — *House Selling For Dummies* and *Mortgages For Dummies*.

Real Estate Investing For Dummies®

Real estate is a proven wealth-building investment, but many people don't know how to go about making and managing rental property investments. Real estate and property management expert Robert Griswold and Eric Tyson cover the gamut of property investment options, strategies, and techniques.

Small Business For Dummies®

Take control of your future, and make the leap from employee to entrepreneur with this enterprising guide. From drafting a business plan to managing costs, you'll profit from expert advice and real-world examples that cover every aspect of building your own business.

Investing in Your 20s & 30s

FOR
DUMMIES®

by Eric Tyson, MBA

WILEY

John Wiley & Sons, Inc.

Investing in Your 20s & 30s For Dummies®
Published by
John Wiley & Sons, Inc.
111 River St.
Hoboken, NJ 07030-5774
www.wiley.com

WILEY

About the Author

Eric Tyson is an internationally acclaimed and best-selling personal finance author, lecturer, speaker, and former advisor. Through his work, he is dedicated to teaching people to manage their money better and to successfully direct their own investments.

Eric is a former management consultant to businesses for which he helped improve operations and profitability. Before, during, and after this time of working crazy hours and traveling too much, he had the good sense to focus on financial matters.

He has been involved in the investing markets in many capacities for more than three decades. Eric first invested in mutual funds back in the mid-1970s, when he opened a mutual fund account at Fidelity. With the assistance of Dr. Martin Zweig, a now-famous investment market analyst, Eric won his high school's science fair in 1976 for a project on what influences the stock market. In addition to investing in securities over the decades, Eric has successfully invested in real estate and started and managed his own business. He has counseled thousands of clients on a variety of investment quandaries and questions.

He earned a bachelor's degree in economics at Yale and an MBA at the Stanford Graduate School of Business. Despite these impediments to lucid reasoning, he came to his senses and decided that life was too short to spend it working long hours and waiting in airports for the benefit of larger companies.

An accomplished freelance personal finance writer, Eric is the author of numerous best-selling books, including *For Dummies* books on personal finance, investing, mutual funds, and home buying (co-author), and is a syndicated columnist. His work has been featured and quoted in hundreds of national and local publications, including *Kiplinger's Personal Finance Magazine, Los Angeles Times, Chicago Tribune, The Wall Street Journal,* and *Bottom Line/Personal,* and on NBC's *Today Show,* ABC, CNBC, PBS's *Nightly Business Report,* FOX, CNN, CBS national radio, Bloomberg Business Radio, National Public Radio, and Business Radio Network. He's also been a featured speaker at a White House conference on retirement planning.

You can visit him on the web at www.erictyson.com.

Dedication

Actually, before I get to the thank yous, please allow me a *really* major thank you and dedication.

This book is hereby and irrevocably dedicated to my family and friends, as well as to my former students, counseling clients, and customers, who ultimately taught me everything I know about how to explain financial terms and strategies so that all of us may benefit.

Author's Acknowledgments

First, I'd like to thank Elizabeth Rea. Thanks also to Kathy Simpson for all of her fine editing and to all of the fine folks in Composition and Graphics for making this book look great! Thanks also to everyone else who contributed to getting this book done well and on time.

And last but not least, a tip of my cap to the fine technical reviewers — Gary Karz and John Nelson — who helped to ensure that I didn't write something that wasn't quite right. . . .

Publisher's Acknowledgments

We're proud of this book; please send us your comments at http://dummies.custhelp.com. For other comments, please contact our Customer Care Department within the U.S. at 877-762-2974, outside the U.S. at 317-572-3993, or fax 317-572-4002.

Some of the people who helped bring this book to market include the following:

Acquisitions, Editorial, and Vertical Websites

Project Editor: Elizabeth Rea

Acquisitions Editor: Erin Calligan Mooney

Copy Editor: Kathy Simpson

Assistant Editor: David Lutton

Editorial Program Coordinator: Joe Niesen

Technical Editors: Gary Karz, CFA; John L. Nelson, CFA

Editorial Manager: Michelle Hacker

Editorial Assistant: Alexa Koschier

Cover Photos: © iStockphoto.com/vova Kalina, © iStockphoto.com/pictafolio

Cartoons: Rich Tennant (www.the5thwave.com)

Composition Services

Project Coordinator: Kristie Rees

Layout and Graphics: Jennifer Creasey, Joyce Haughey, Laura Westhuis

Proofreaders: Cynthia Fields, Lauren Mandelbaum

Indexer: Dakota Indexing

Publishing and Editorial for Consumer Dummies

Kathleen Nebenhaus, Vice President and Executive Publisher

David Palmer, Associate Publisher

Kristin Ferguson-Wagstaffe, Product Development Director

Publishing for Technology Dummies

Andy Cummings, Vice President and Publisher

Composition Services

Debbie Stailey, Director of Composition Services

Contents at a Glance

Table of Contents

Introduction

*I*nvesting offers so many possibilities and so many choices.

Your young adult years, which at least for the purposes of this book I define as your 20s and 30s, are filled with so much promise and potential. Your career, your interests, your personal life, and your family and friends all compete for your time and attention.

Most folks work upward of 2,000 hours per year earning a living. Managing the money that passes through their hands is an important task, which most folks aren't trained to do.

Earning money generally takes a lot of work. Managing your personal finances and saving money take discipline and sacrifice. When you have money to invest, you want to do the best that you can so that you earn a decent return without ending up in failed investments.

About This Book

I designed and wrote this book to help you with the important and challenging task of investing. Your young adult years are a great time to lay the best foundation for investing wisely. After all, some of the investments you make now and in the near future will have decades to grow and multiply.

I've worked with and taught people from all financial situations, so I know the investing concerns and questions of real folks just like you. I've discovered how important having healthy and strong personal finances and investments is.

I first became interested in money matters as a middle-school student when my father was laid off and received some retirement money. I worked with my dad to make investing decisions with the money. A couple of years later, I won my high school's science fair with a project on what influences the stock market.

During my younger adult years, I worked hard to keep my living expenses low and to save and invest money so that I could leave my job and pursue my entrepreneurial ideas. I accomplished that goal in my late 20s. I hope to give you some tools to help you make the most of your money and investments so you too can meet your goals and dreams.

Conventions Used in This Book

To help you navigate the waters of this book, I've set up a few conventions:

- ✔ I use *italics* for emphasis and to highlight new words or terms that I define.

- ✔ I use **boldface** text to indicate the action part of numbered steps and to highlight key words or phrases in bulleted lists.

- ✔ I put all web addresses in monofont for easy identification.

What You're Not to Read

I've written this book so you can find information easily and easily understand what you find. And although I'd like to believe that you want to pore over every last word between the two yellow-and-black covers, I actually make it easy for you to identify "skippable" material. The sidebars are the shaded boxes that appear here and there. They include helpful information and observations that, while interesting, aren't essential for you to know.

Foolish Assumptions

No matter what your current situation is — whether you're entering the job market right after high school, graduating college with a large amount of student loans, pretty well established in your career, and so on — I thought of you as I wrote this book and made some assumptions about you:

✔ You want expert advice about important investing topics such as getting a preinvesting financial checkup, understanding the range of investments available, and assembling a killer investment portfolio. And you want that advice quickly.

✔ You want a crash course in investing and are looking for a book you can read cover to cover to help solidify major concepts and get you thinking about your investments in a more comprehensive way.

✔ You're tired of feeling overwhelmed by your investing choices and stressed out by the ever-changing economic and investing landscape, and you want to get more comfortable with your investment selections.

This book is basic enough to help a novice get his or her arms around thorny investing issues. But advanced readers will be challenged as well to think about their investments and finances in a new way and identify areas for improvement. Check out the table of contents for a chapter-by-chapter rundown of what this book offers. You can also look up a specific topic in the index. Or you can turn a few pages and start at the beginning: Chapter 1.

How This Book Is Organized

Investing in Your 20s and 30s For Dummies is organized into five parts, with each covering a major area of investing. The chapters within each part focus on specific elements or avenues of investing in detail. Here are the highlights of what you can find in each part.

Part 1: Understanding Investing Terms and Concepts

In this part, I help you make sense of all the investing lingo that's out there, including understanding folks who claim to be able to help you make investing decisions. I also explain how to set and achieve common goals with your investments. This part closes by discussing the reasonable returns to expect from various investments, how those returns compound over time, how taxes work on investments, and what you can do to minimize your investment taxes.

Part II: Preparing Your Investing Foundation

In this part, I explain how your financial plans should translate into your investing plans and what financial housekeeping you should do before investing. I also explain what role bank and credit union accounts can play in your investment portfolio and what alternatives can make you more money. Finally, I discuss money market mutual funds and how to select the right one for your situation.

Part III: Beginning Investments

You don't already have to be rich to tap into the best investments! In this part, I explain how stocks and bonds work and how to make money in them. I also cover fund investing — specifically, investing in mutual funds and exchange-traded funds. I discuss how to match funds to your objectives, how to create and manage a fund portfolio, and how to choose among alternatives to funds.

Part IV: Advanced Investments

This part covers more advanced and complicated investments that you should consider. I start with real estate, which not only could include a home in which you live, but also investment property you would rent out. Then I move on to small-business investing, which can include starting your own company, buying a company, and possibly investing in someone else's company. I close by discussing some other investments, including annuities, insurance, collectibles, gold, and other commodities.

Part V: The Part of Tens

In this part, I present some lists of ten-somethings that can help you with your finances. The topics covered are the ten things you need to know about information resources and the ten principles of investing success.

Icons Used in This Book

The icons in this book help you find particular kinds of information that may be of use to you:

This target marks strategy recommendations for making the most of your investments.

This icon points out information that you'll definitely want to remember.

This icon marks things to avoid and points out common mistakes people make when making and managing their investments.

This icon alerts you to scams and scoundrels who prey on the unsuspecting.

This icon tells you when you should consider doing some additional research. Don't worry — I explain what to look for and what to look out for.

Where to Go from Here

This book is organized so you can go wherever you want to find complete information. You can use the table of contents to find broad categories of information or the index to look up more specific topics.

If you're not sure where you want to go, you may want to start with Part I. It gives you all the basic info you need to assess your financial and investing situation and points to places where you can find more detailed information for improving it.

Part I

Understanding Investing Terms and Concepts

The 5th Wave   By Rich Tennant

"You're 22 years old, you want to invest your money – let's talk some smack."

In this part...

1 cover conceptual material starting with defining commonly used investing jargon, including explaining the different types of investments, along with their expected returns and risks. I also delve into how to use investments to accomplish your goals, such as making larger purchases, buying a home, and investing for retirement. Lastly, I discuss how investment returns are taxed and what you can legally do to minimize your taxes on your investments.

Chapter 1

Making Sense of Your Investing Options

. . . .

In This Chapter

▶ Common investments and how they compare

▶ Investment terminology explained — risks and returns

▶ The gobbledygook of professionals, credentials, and investment companies

. . . .

*S*o many fields and disciplines are packed full of jargon. Some of this is the result of "progress" and advances, and some of it is caused by workers in the field not going out of their way enough to explain and define things.

In this chapter, I give you the lay of the land regarding the enormous numbers of choices and foreign-sounding terminology that await you in the world of investing. I also explain the types of companies that offer investments and their strengths and weaknesses. And should you want to hire some investing help, I also detail the various professionals pitching their services to you and the common credentials they hawk to convince you of their expertise.

Growing Your Money in Ownership Investments

The most exciting thing about investing during your younger adult years is that you can be more aggressive with money that you've earmarked to help you accomplish long-term goals. To achieve typical longer-term financial goals, such as retiring, the money that you save and invest generally needs to grow at a rate much faster than the rate of inflation. If you put your money in a bank account that pays little or no interest, for example, you're likely to fall short of your goals.

Ownership investments are investments like stocks, where you own a piece of a company, real estate, or a small business that has the capability to generate revenue and profits. Over the long term, consider ownership investments if you want your money to grow much faster than the rate of inflation and don't mind more volatility in your investments' values.

The downside to such investments is that they can fall more significantly in value than non-ownership investments, especially in the short term. So don't put money into ownership investments that you may need to tap in the short term for rent money or your next vacation. To reduce the risk of ownership investments, *diversify* — that is, hold different types of ownership investments that don't move in tandem.

I cover three major ownership investments in the following sections: stocks, real estate, and small business.

Sharing in corporate growth and profits: Stocks

If you want the potential to share in the growth and profits of companies, you can gain it through buying shares of their stock. Stocks are shares of ownership in a company. You can buy stock directly in individual companies through a brokerage account, or you can buy a collection of stocks via a mutual fund or exchange-traded fund (see Chapter 10).

You don't need to be a business genius to make money in stocks. Simply make regular and systematic investments, and invest in proven companies and funds while minimizing your investment expenses and taxes. Of course, there's no guarantee that every stock or stock fund that you buy will increase in value. In Chapter 8, I explain proven and time-tested methods for making money in stocks.

Profiting from real estate

You don't need to be a high roller to make money investing in real estate. Owning and managing real estate is like running a small business: You need to satisfy customers (tenants), manage your costs, keep an eye on the competition, and so on. Some methods of real estate investing require more time than others, but many are proven ways to build wealth.

Among the key attributes of real estate investment are the following:

- ✔ You build wealth through your rental income exceeding your expenses and through property-value appreciation.
- ✔ You can leverage your investment by borrowing money.
- ✔ You must be comfortable dealing with property management, which includes finding and retaining tenants and keeping up (and possibly improving) your property.

See Chapter 11 for the details on investing in real estate.

Succeeding in small business

I know people who have hit investing home runs by owning or buying businesses. Most people work full-time at running their businesses, increasing their chances of doing something big financially with them. Investing in the stock market, by contrast, tends to be more part-time in nature.

In addition to the financial rewards, however, small-business owners can enjoy seeing the impact of their work and knowing that it makes a difference. I can speak from firsthand experience (as can other small-business owners) in saying that emotionally and financially, entrepreneurship is a roller coaster.

Besides starting your own company, you can share in the economic rewards of the entrepreneurial world through buying an existing business or investing in someone else's budding enterprise. See Chapter 12 for more details.

Keeping Money in Lending Investments

In the first section of this chapter, "Growing Your Money in Ownership Investments," I discuss how you can make your dough grow much faster than the cost of living by using stocks, real estate, and small business. However, you may want or need to play it safer when investing money for shorter-term purposes, so you should then consider lending investments. Many people use such investments through local banks, such as in a checking account, savings account, or certificate of deposit. In all these cases with a bank, you're lending your money to the bank.

Another lending investment is bonds. When you purchase a bond that has been issued by the government or a company, you agree to lend your money for a predetermined period of time and receive a particular rate of interest. A corporate bond may pay you 4 percent interest over the next three years, for example.

An investor's return from lending investments is typically limited to the original investment plus interest payments. If you lend your money to a company through one of its bonds that matures in, say, five years, and the firm doubles its revenue and profits over that period, you won't share in its growth. The company's stockholders reap the rewards of the company's success, but as a bondholder, you don't. You simply get interest and the face value of the bond back at maturity.

Similar to bank savings accounts, money market mutual funds are another type of lending investment. Money market mutual funds generally invest in ultra-safe things such as short-term bank certificates of deposit, U.S. government–issued Treasury bills, and commercial paper (short-term bonds) that the most creditworthy corporations issue.

Many people keep too much of their money in lending investments, thus allowing others to reap the rewards of economic growth. Although lending investments appear safer because you know in advance what return you'll receive, they aren't that safe. The long-term risk of these seemingly safe money investments is that your money will grow too slowly to enable you to accomplish your personal financial goals. In the worst cases, the company or other institution to which you're lending money can go under and fail to repay your loan.

Understanding Risks and Returns

Who among us wants to lose money? Of course you don't! You put your money into an investment in the hope and expectation that you will get back more in total than you put in. When it comes to investing, no concepts are more important to grasp than *risk* and *return*, which I explain in this section.

Understanding risks

The investments that you expect to produce higher returns fluctuate more in value, particularly in the short term. However, if you attempt to avoid all the risks involved in investing, you likely won't succeed, and you likely won't be happy with your investment results and lifestyle. In the investment world, some people don't go near stocks or real estate that they perceive to be volatile, for example. As a result, such investors often end up with lousy long-term returns and expose themselves to some high risks that they overlooked, such as the risk of inflation and taxes eroding the purchasing power of their money.

You can't live without taking risks. Risk-free activities or ways of living don't exist. You can sensibly minimize risks, but you can never eliminate them. Some methods of risk reduction aren't palatable because they reduce your quality of life.

Risks are also composed of several factors. Following are the major types of investment risks and a few of the methods you can use to reduce these risks while not missing out on the upside that investments offer:

✔ **Market-value risk:** Although stocks can help you build wealth, they can also drop 20 percent or more in a relatively short period of time. Although real estate, like stocks, has been a rewarding long-term investment, various real estate markets get clobbered from time to time.

✔ **Individual-investment risk:** A down market can put an entire investment market on a roller-coaster ride, but healthy markets also have their share of individual losers. Just as individual stock prices can plummet, so can individual real estate property prices.

✔ **Purchasing-power risk:** *Inflation* — which is an increase in the cost of living — can erode the value of your money and its *purchasing power* (what you can buy with that money). I often see skittish investors keep their money in bonds and money market accounts, thinking that they're playing it safe. The risk in this strategy is that your money won't grow enough over the years for you to accomplish your financial goals. In other words, the lower the return you earn, the more you need to save to reach a financial goal. As a younger investor, you need to pay the most attention to the risk of generating low returns because your money will be invested over so many years and decades.

With lending investments, you have a claim on a specific amount of a currency. Occasionally, currencies falter. This is a low frequency but very high impact risk that most folks ignore when thinking about lending investments.

✔ **Liquidity risk:** Some investments are more liquid than others and more readily sold at fair market value on short notice. Bank savings accounts have no real liquidity risk. A real estate investment, by contrast, takes time and money to sell, and if you must sell most real estate quickly, you'll likely get a fair amount less than its current full market value.

✔ **Career risk:** In your 20s and 30s, your ability to earn money is probably your biggest asset. Education is a lifelong process. If you don't continually invest in your education, you risk losing your competitive edge. Your skills and perspectives can become dated and obsolete. Although that doesn't mean you should work 80 hours a week and never do anything fun, it does mean that part of your "work" time should involve upgrading your skills.

Managing risks

Throughout this book as I discuss various investments, I explain how to get the most out of each one. Because I've introduced the important issue of risk in this chapter, I would be remiss if I also didn't give you some early ideas about how to minimize those risks. Here are some simple steps you can take to lower the risk of investments that can upset the achievement of your goals:

- ✔ **Do your homework.** When you purchase real estate, a whole host of inspections can save you from buying a money pit. With stocks, you can examine some measures of value and the company's financial condition and business strategy to reduce your chances of buying into an over-priced company or one on the verge of major problems.

- ✔ **Diversify.** Placing significant amounts of your capital in one or a handful of securities is risky, particularly if the stocks are in the same industry or closely related indus-tries. To reduce this risk, purchase stocks in a variety of industries and companies within each industry. Even better is buying diversified mutual funds and exchange-traded funds. Diversifying your investments can involve more than just your stock portfolio. You can also hold some real estate investments to diversify your invest-ment portfolio.

  If you worry about the health of the U.S. economy, the government, and the dollar, you can reduce your invest-ment risk by investing overseas. Most large U.S. compa-nies do business overseas, so when you invest in larger U.S. company stocks, you get some international invest-ment exposure. You can also invest in international com-pany stocks, ideally through funds.

- ✔ **Minimize holdings in costly markets.** Although I don't believe that most investors can time the markets — buy low, sell high — spotting a greatly overpriced market isn't too difficult. You should avoid overpriced invest-ments because when they fall, they usually fall farther and faster than more fairly priced investments. Also, you should be able to find other investments that offer higher potential returns. Throughout this book, I explain some simple yet powerful methods you can use to measure whether a particular investment market is of fair value, of good value, or overpriced.

- ✔ **View market declines in a different light.** Instead of seeing declines and market corrections as horrible things, view them as potential opportunities or "sales." If you pass up the stock and real estate markets simply because of the potential market-value risk, you miss out on a historic, time-tested method of building substantial wealth. Try not to give in to the human emotions that often scare people away from buying something that others seem to be shunning.

Making sense of returns

Each investment has its own mix of associated risks that you take when you part with your investment dollar and, likewise, offers a different potential rate of return. When you make investments, you have the potential to make money in a variety of ways.

To determine how much money you've made or lost on your investment, you need to calculate the total return. To come up with this figure, you need to determine how much money you originally invested and then factor in the other components, such as interest, dividends, and appreciation or depreciation.

If you've ever had money in a bank account that pays interest, you know that the bank pays you a small amount of interest when you allow it to keep your money. The bank then turns around and lends your money to some other person or organization at a much higher rate of interest. The rate of interest is also known as the *yield.* So if a bank tells you that its savings account pays 2 percent interest, the bank may also say that the account yields 2 percent. Banks usually quote interest rates or yields on an annual basis. Interest that you receive is one component of the return you receive on your investment.

If a bank pays monthly interest, the bank also likely quotes a compounded effective annual yield. After the first month's interest is credited to your account, that interest starts earning interest as well. So the bank may say that the account pays 1 percent, which compounds to an effective annual yield of 1.02 percent.

When you lend your money directly to a company — which is what you do when you invest in a bond that a corporation issues — you also receive interest. Bonds, as well as stocks (which are shares of ownership in a company), fluctuate in market value after they're issued.

When you invest in a company's stock, you hope that the stock increases (appreciates) in value. Of course, a stock can also decline, or depreciate, in value. This change in market value is part of your return from a stock or bond investment.

Stocks can also pay dividends, which are the company's way of sharing of some of its profits with you as a stockholder and thus are part of your return. Some companies, particularly those that are small or growing rapidly, choose to reinvest all their profits back into the company.

Unless you held your investments in a tax-sheltered retirement account, you owe taxes on your return. Specifically, the dividends and investment appreciation that you realize upon selling are taxed, although often at relatively low rates. The tax rates on so-called long-term capital gains and stock dividends are currently and historically lower than the tax rates on other income. I discuss the different tax rates that affect your investments and explain how to make tax-wise investment decisions that fit with your overall personal financial situation and goals in Chapter 4.

Where to Invest and Get Advice

Discussing the companies through which you can invest and where to get investing advice may seem out of place to you if you started reading this book from the beginning. But I'm doing this because I strongly believe that you should begin to think about and understand the lay of the land in these important areas so that you can make the best choices.

Selecting the firm or firms through which to do your investing is a hugely important decision. So is the decision about from whom to get or pay for investing advice. In this section, I address both of these topics.

Finding the best fund companies and brokers

Insurance companies, banks, investment brokerage firms, mutual funds — the list of companies that stand ready to help you invest your money is nearly endless. Most people stumble into a relationship with an investment firm. They may choose a company because their employer uses it for company retirement plans or they've read about or been recommended to a particular company.

When you invest in certain securities — such as stocks and bonds and exchange-traded funds (ETFs) — and when you want to hold mutual funds from different companies in a single account, you need brokerage services. Brokers execute your trades to buy or sell stocks, bonds, and other securities and enable you to centralize your holdings of mutual funds, ETFs, and other investments. Your broker can also assist you with other services that may interest you.

Deciding which investment company is best for you depends on your needs and wants. In addition to fees, consider how important having a local branch office is to you. If you want to invest in mutual funds, you'll want to choose a firm that offers access to good funds, including money market funds in which you can deposit money awaiting investment or proceeds from a sale.

For the lowest trading commissions, you generally must place your trades online. But you should be careful. A low brokerage fee of, say, $7 or $10 per trade doesn't really save you money if you trade a lot and rack up significant total commissions. Also you pay more in taxes when you trade more frequently and realize shorter-term (one year or less) profits.

Trading online is an easy way to act impulsively and emotionally when making important investment decisions. If you're prone to such actions, or if you find yourself tracking and trading investments too closely, stay away from this form of trading, and use the Internet only to check account information and gather factual information. Increasing numbers of brokers offer account information and trading capabilities via personal digital assistants, which, of course, add to your costs. Digital assistants can also promote addictive investment behaviors.

Among my top investment firm selections are firms that offer mutual funds and ETFs and/or brokerage services.

Broker	Phone Number	Website
E*Trade	800-387-2331	https://us.etrade.com
Muriel Siebert	800-872-0711	www.siebertnet.com/index.aspx
Scottrade	800-619-7283	www.scottrade.com
T. Rowe Price	800-638-5660	www.troweprice.com
Vanguard	800-992-8327	www.vanguard.com
TD Ameritrade	800-934-4448	www.tdameritrade.com

Finding an admirable advisor

I would always counsel folks who took personal finance courses I taught or who contacted me seeking advice to get educated before engaging the services of any financial advisor. How can you possibly evaluate the competence of someone you may hire if you yourself are financially clueless? You've got this book, so read it before you consider hiring someone for financial advice.

By taking the themes and major concepts of this book to heart, you'll greatly minimize your chances of making significant investment blunders, including hiring an incompetent or unethical advisor. You might be tempted, for example, to retain the services of an advisor who claims that he and his firm can predict the future economic environment and position your portfolio to take advantage. But you'll find in reading this book that financial advisors don't have crystal balls and that you should steer clear of folks who purport to be able jump into and out of investments based upon their forecasts.

Finding a competent and objective financial advisor isn't easy. Historically, most financial consultants work on commission, and the promise of that commission can cloud their judgment. Among the minority of fee-based advisors, almost all manage money, which creates other conflicts of interest. The more money you give them to invest and manage, the more money these advisors make. That's why I generally prefer seeking financial (and tax) advice from advisors who sell their time (on an hourly basis) and don't sell anything else.

Because investment decisions are a critical part of financial planning, take note of the fact that the most-common designations of educational training among professional money managers are MBA (master of business administration) and CFA (chartered financial analyst). Financial planners often have the CFP (certified financial planner) credential, and some tax advisors who work on an hourly basis have the PFS (personal financial specialist) credential.

Advisors who provide investment advice and oversee at least $100 million must register with the U.S. Securities and Exchange Commission (SEC); otherwise, they generally register with the state that they make their principal place of business. They must file Form ADV, otherwise known as the Uniform Application for Investment Adviser Registration. This lengthy document asks investment advisors to provide in a uniform format such details as a breakdown of where their income comes from, their education and employment history, the types of securities the advisory firm recommends, and the advisor's fee schedule.

You can ask the advisor to send you a copy of his Form ADV. You can also find out whether the advisor is registered and whether he has a track record of problems by calling the SEC at 800-732-0330 or by visiting its website at www.adviserinfo. sec.gov. Many states require the registration of financial advisors, so you should also contact the department that oversees advisors in your state. Visit the North American Securities Administrators Association's website (www.nasaa.org), and click the Contact Your Regulator link on the home page.

Chapter 2

Using Investments to Accomplish Your Goals

*S*aving and investing money can make you feel good and in control. Ultimately, most folks are investing money to accomplish particular goals. Saving and investing for a car purchase, expenses for higher education, a home purchase, new furniture, or a vacation are typical short-term goals. You can also invest toward longer-term goals, such as retirement decades in the future.

In this chapter, I discuss how you can use investments to accomplish common shorter- and longer-term goals.

Setting and Prioritizing Your Shorter-Term Goals

Unless you earn really big bucks or expect to have a large family inheritance to tap, your personal and financial desires will probably outstrip your resources. Thus, you must prioritize your goals.

One of the biggest mistakes I see people make is rushing into a financial decision without considering what's really important to them. Because many people get caught up in the responsibilities of their daily lives, they often don't have time for reflection. Take that time, because people who identify their goals and then work toward them, which often requires changing some habits, are the ones who accomplish their goals.

In this section, I discuss common "shorter-term" financial goals — such as establishing an emergency reserve, making major purchases, owning a home, and starting a small business — and how to work toward them. Accomplishing such goals almost always requires saving money.

Accumulating a rainy-day fund

The future is unpredictable. Take the uncertainty simply surrounding your job: You could lose your job, or you might want to leave it. Because you don't know what the future holds, preparing for the unexpected is financially wise. Enter the emergency or rainy-day fund.

The size of your emergency fund depends on your personal situation. Begin by considering how much you spend in a typical month. Here are some benchmarks for how many months' worth of living expenses you should have:

- ✔ **Three months' living expenses:** When you're starting out, this minimalist approach makes sense if your only current source of emergency funds is a high-interest credit card. Longer-term, you could make do with three months' living expenses if you have other accounts, such as a 401(k), or family members and close friends whom you can tap for a short-term loan.

- ✔ **Six months' living expenses:** If you don't have other places to turn for a loan, or if you have some instability in your employment situation or source of income, you need more of a cushion.

- ✔ **Twelve months' living expenses:** Consider this large a stash if your income fluctuates greatly or if your occupation involves a high risk of job loss, finding another job could take you a long time, or you don't have other places to turn for a loan.

Saving for large purchases

Most people want things — such as furniture, a vacation, or a car — that they don't have cash on hand to pay for. I strongly advise saving for your larger consumer purchases to avoid paying for them over time with high-interest consumer credit. Don't take out credit card or auto loans — otherwise known as *consumer credit* — to make large purchases. (Don't be duped by a seemingly low interest rate on, for example, a car loan. You could get the car at a lower price if you don't opt for such a loan.)

 Paying for high-interest consumer debt can undermine your ability to save toward your goals and your ability to make major purchases in the future. Don't deny yourself gratification; just figure out how to delay it. When contemplating the purchase of a consumer item on credit, add up the total interest you'd end up paying on your debt, and call it the price of instant gratification.

Investing for a small business or home

In your early years of saving and investing, deciding whether to save money to buy a home or to put money into a retirement account presents a dilemma. In the long run, owning your own home is usually a wise financial move. On the other hand, saving sooner for retirement makes achieving your goals easier and reduces your income tax bill.

Presuming that both goals are important to you, you can save toward both goals: buying a home and retiring. If you're eager to own a home, you can throw all your savings toward achieving that goal and temporarily put your retirement savings on hold.

 You can make penalty-free withdrawals of up to $10,000 from Individual Retirement Accounts (IRAs) toward a first-time home purchase. You might also be able to have the best of both worlds if you work for an employer that allows borrowing against retirement account balances. You can save money in the retirement account and then borrow against it for the down payment on a home. Consider this option with great care, though, because retirement account loans generally must be repaid within a few years or when you quit or lose your job (ask your employer for the details).

When saving money for starting or buying a business, most people encounter the same dilemma they face when deciding to save to buy a house: If you fund your retirement accounts to the exclusion of earmarking money for your small-business dreams, your entrepreneurial aspirations may never become reality. Generally, I advocate hedging your bets by saving money in your tax-sheltered retirement accounts as well as toward your business venture. An investment in your own small business can produce great rewards, so you may feel comfortable focusing your savings on your own business.

Saving for kids' educational costs

Do you have little ones or plan to have them in your future? You probably know that rearing a child (or two) costs really big bucks. But the biggest expense awaits when they reach young adulthood and want to go to college, so your instincts may be to try to save money to accomplish and afford that goal.

The college financial-aid system effectively penalizes you for saving money outside retirement accounts and penalizes you even more if the money is invested in the child's name. Wanting to provide for your children's future is perfectly natural, but doing so before you've saved adequately toward your own goals can be a major financial mistake.

This concept may sound selfish, but the reality is that you need to take care of *your* future first. Take advantage of saving through your tax-sheltered retirement accounts before you set aside money in custodial savings accounts for your kids.

Investing short-term money

So where should you invest money earmarked for a shorter-term goal? A money market account or short-term bond fund is a good place to store your short-term savings. See Chapters 7 and 9 for more information on these options. The best bank or credit union accounts (covered in Chapter 6) may be worth considering as well.

Investing in Retirement Accounts

During your younger adult years, you may not be thinking much about retirement, because it seems to be well off in the distance. But if you'd like to scale back on your work schedule someday, partly or completely, you're best off saving toward that goal as soon as you start drawing a regular paycheck.

In this section, I explain the benefits and possible concerns of investing through so-called retirement accounts. I also lay out the retirement account options you may access.

Understanding retirement account perks

Where possible, try to save and invest in accounts that offer you a tax advantage, which is precisely what retirement accounts offer you. These accounts — known by such enlightening acronyms and names as 401(k), 403(b), SEP-IRA, Keogh, and so on — offer tax breaks to people of all economic means. Consider the following advantages to investing in retirement accounts:

- ✔ **Contributions often provide up-front tax breaks.** By investing through a retirement account, you not only plan wisely for your future, but you also get an immediate financial reward: lower taxes, which mean more money available for saving and investing. Retirement account contributions generally aren't taxed at either the federal or state income tax level until withdrawal (but they're still subject to Social Security and Medicare taxes when earned). If you're paying, say, 30 percent between federal and state taxes (see Chapter 4 to determine your tax bracket), a $4,000 contribution to a retirement account lowers your taxes by $1,200.

  Modest income earners also may get an additional government tax credit known as the Retirement Savings Contributions Credit. A maximum credit of 50 percent applies to the first $2,000 contributed for single taxpayers with an adjusted gross income (AGI) of no more than

$17,250 and married couples filing jointly with an AGI of $34,500 or less. Singles with an AGI of between $17,250 and $18,750 and married couples with an AGI between $34,500 and $37,500 are eligible for a 20 percent tax credit. Single taxpayers with an AGI of more than $18,750 but no more than $28,750, as well as married couples with an AGI between $37,500 and $57,500, can get a 10 percent tax credit.

✔ **Your employer may match some of your contributions.** This money is free money from your employer, and it's use it or lose it, so don't miss out!

✔ **Investment returns compound tax-free.** After you put money into a retirement account, you get to defer taxes on all the accumulating gains and profits (including interest and dividends) until you withdraw the money down the road. Thus, more money is working for you over a longer period of time. (One exception: Roth IRAs offer no up-front tax breaks but permit tax-free withdrawal of investment earnings in retirement.)

Grappling with retirement account concerns

There are legitimate concerns about putting money into a retirement account. First and foremost is the fact that once you place such money inside a retirement account, you can't access it before age 59½ without paying current income taxes and a penalty — 10 percent of the withdrawn amount in federal tax, plus whatever your state charges.

This poses a problem on several levels. First, money placed inside retirement accounts is generally not available for other uses, such as buying a car or starting a small business. Second, if an emergency arises and you need to tap the money, you'll get socked with taxes and penalties.

You can use the following ways to avoid the early-withdrawal penalties that the tax authorities normally apply:

✔ You can make penalty-free withdrawals of up to $10,000 from IRAs for a first-time home purchase or higher educational expenses for you, your spouse, or your children (and even grandchildren).

> ✔ Some company retirement plans allow you to borrow
> against your balance. You're essentially loaning money to
> yourself, with the interest payments going back into your
> account.
>
> ✔ If you have major medical expenses (exceeding 7.5 per-
> cent of your income) or a disability, you may be exempt
> from the penalties under certain conditions. (You will
> still owe ordinary income tax on withdrawals.)
>
> ✔ You may withdraw money before age 59½ if you do so in
> equal, annual installments based on your life expectancy.
> You generally must make such distributions for at least
> five years or until age 59½, whichever is later.

If you lose your job and withdraw retirement account money
simply because you need it to live on, the penalties do apply.
If you're not working, however, and you're earning so little
income that you need to tap your retirement account, you
would likely be in a low tax bracket. The lower income taxes
you pay (compared with the taxes you would have paid on
that money had you not sheltered it in a retirement account
in the first place) should make up for most, if not all, of the
penalty.

But what about simply wanting to save money for nearer-term
goals and to be able to tap that money? If you're saving and
investing money for a down payment on a home or to start
a business, for example, you'll probably need to save that
money outside a retirement account to avoid those early-
withdrawal penalties.

If you're like most folks and have limited financial resources,
you need to prioritize your goals. Before funding retirement
accounts and gaining those tax breaks, be sure to contemplate and prioritize your other goals (see the section "Setting
and Prioritizing Your Shorter-Term Goals," earlier in this
chapter).

Taking advantage of retirement accounts

To take advantage of retirement savings plans and the tax
savings that accompany them, you must spend less than you

earn. Only then can you afford to contribute to these retirement savings plans, unless you already happen to have a stash of cash from previous savings or an inheritance.

The common mistake that many younger adults make is neglecting to take advantage of retirement accounts because of their enthusiasm for spending or investing in nonretirement accounts. Not investing in tax-sheltered retirement accounts can cost you hundreds, perhaps thousands, of dollars per year in lost tax savings. Add that loss up over the many years that you work and save, and not taking advantage of these tax reduction accounts can easily cost you tens of thousands to hundreds of thousands of dollars in the long term.

The sooner you start to save, the less painful it is each year to save enough to reach your goals, because your contributions have more years to compound. Each decade you delay saving approximately doubles the percentage of your earnings that you need to save to meet your goals. If saving 5 percent per year in your early 20s gets you to your retirement goal, waiting until your 30s to start may mean socking away 10 percent to reach that same goal; waiting until your 40s means saving 20 percent.

Surveying retirement account choices

If you earn employment income (or receive alimony), you have options for putting money away in a retirement account that compounds without taxation until you withdraw the money. In most cases, your contributions to these retirement accounts are tax-deductible. This section reviews your options.

Company-based retirement plans

Larger for-profit companies generally offer their employees a *401(k)* plan, which typically allows saving up to $17,000 per year (for tax year 2012). Many nonprofit organizations offer their employees similar plans, known as *403(b)* plans. Contributions to both traditional 401(k) and 403(b) plans are deductible on both your federal and state taxes in the year that you make them. Employees of nonprofit organizations can generally contribute up to 20 percent or $17,000 of their salaries, whichever is less.

Figuring how much to save for retirement

Among the mass market website tools and booklets focused on retirement planning, I like T. Rowe Price's Retirement Income Calculator available online at www3.trowe price.com/ric/ricweb/ public/ric.do. It walks you through the calculations needed to figure how much you should be saving to reach your retirement goal.

The assumptions that you plug into this calculator are really important, so here's a review of the key ones:

✔ **Asset allocation:** Enter your current allocation and then select an allocation for after you're retired. For the retirement allocation, you can choose a fixed combination of 40 percent stock, 40 percent bond, 20 percent money market fund. The calculator doesn't include real estate as a possible asset. If you own real estate as an investment, you should treat those assets as a stock-like investment, since they have similar long-term risk and return characteristics. (Calculate your equity in investment real estate, which is the difference between a property's current market value and mortgage debt on that property.)

✔ **Age of retirement:** Plug in your preferred age of retirement, within reason, of course. There's no point plugging in a dream number like "I'd like to retire by age 45, but I know the only way I can do that

is to win the lottery!" Depending upon how the analysis works out, you can always go back and plug in a different age. Sometimes folks are pleasantly surprised that their combined accumulated resources provide them with a decent enough standard of living that they can consider retiring sooner than they thought.

✔ **Include Social Security?:** T. Rowe's calculator asks if you want to include expected Social Security benefits. I'd rather that they didn't pose this question at all, because you definitely should include your Social Security benefits in the calculations. Don't buy into the nonsense that the Social Security program will vaporize and you'll get little to nothing from it. For the vast majority of people, Social Security benefits are an important component of their retirement income, so do include it. Based upon your current income, T. Rowe Price's program will automatically plug in your estimated benefits. So long as your income hasn't changed or won't change dramatically, using the calculator's estimated number should be fine. Alternatively, you could use a recent Social Security Benefits Statement if you have one handy, or visit the Social Security website.

(continued)

(continued)

Price's analysis allows to you make adjustments such as your desired age of retirement, rate of savings, and to what age you'd like your savings to last. So, for example, if the analysis shows that you have much more than enough to retire by age 65, try plugging in, say, age 62 and voilà, the calculator quickly shows you how the numbers change.

There's a benefit in addition to the up-front and ongoing tax benefits of these retirement savings plans: Some employers match your contributions. (If you're an employee in a small business, you cannot establish your own SEP-IRA or Keogh.) Of course, the challenge for many people is to reduce their spending enough to be able to sock away these kinds of contributions.

Some employers are offering a Roth 401(k) account, which, like a Roth IRA (discussed in the next section), offers employees the ability to contribute on an after-tax basis. Withdrawals from such accounts generally aren't taxed in retirement.

If you're self-employed, you can establish your own retirement savings plans for yourself and any employees you have. *Simplified Employee Pension-Individual Retirement Accounts* (SEP-IRA) and *Keogh* plans allow you to put away up to 20 percent of your self-employment income up to an annual maximum of $50,000 (for tax year 2012).

Keogh plans require more paperwork to set up and administer than SEP-IRAs do. Unlike SEP-IRAs, Keogh plans allow *vesting schedules* that require employees to remain with the company for a certain number of years before they earn the right to access their retirement account balances.

Individual Retirement Accounts

If you work for a company that doesn't offer a retirement savings plan, or if you've exhausted contributions to your company's plan, consider an *Individual Retirement Account* (IRA). Anyone who earns employment income or receives alimony may contribute up to $5,000 annually to an IRA (or the amount of your employment income or alimony income, if it's less than $5,000 in a year). A nonworking spouse may contribute up to $5,000 annually to a spousal IRA.

Your contributions to an IRA may or may not be tax-deductible. For tax year 2012, if you're single and your adjusted gross income is $58,000 or less for the year, you can deduct your full IRA contribution. If you're married and you file your taxes jointly, you're entitled to a full IRA deduction if your AGI is $92,000 per year or less.

If you can't deduct your contribution to a standard IRA account, consider making a contribution to a nondeductible IRA account called the *Roth IRA*. Single taxpayers with an AGI less than $110,000 and joint filers with an AGI less than $173,000 can contribute up to $5,000 per year to a Roth IRA. Although the contribution isn't deductible, earnings inside the account are shielded from taxes, and unlike withdrawals from a standard IRA, qualified withdrawals from a Roth IRA account are free from income tax.

Annuities: Maxing out your retirement savings

What if you have so much cash sitting around that after maxing out your contributions to retirement accounts, including your IRA, you still want to sock more away into a tax-advantaged account? Enter the annuity. *Annuities* are contracts that insurance companies back. If you, the investor (annuity holder), should die during the so-called accumulation phase (that is, before receiving payments from the annuity), your designated beneficiary is guaranteed reimbursement of the amount of your original investment.

Annuities, like IRAs, allow your capital to grow and compound tax-deferred. You defer taxes until you withdraw the money. Unlike an IRA, which has an annual contribution limit of a few thousand dollars, an annuity allows you to deposit as much as you want in any year — even millions of dollars, if you've got millions! As with a Roth IRA, however, you get no up-front tax deduction for your contributions.

Because annuity contributions aren't tax-deductible, and because annuities carry higher annual operating fees to pay for the small amount of insurance that comes with them, don't consider contributing to one until you've fully exhausted your other retirement account investing options. Because of their higher annual expenses, annuities generally make sense only if you won't need the money for 15 or more years.

Selecting retirement account investments

When you establish a retirement account, you may not real-ize that the retirement account is simply a shell or shield that keeps the federal, state, and local governments from taxing your investment earnings each year. You still must choose what investments you want to hold inside your retirement account shell.

You may invest the money in your IRA or self-employed plan retirement account (SEP-IRAs, Keoghs, and so on) in stocks, bonds, mutual funds, and even bank accounts. Mutual funds (offered in most employer-based plans) and exchange-traded funds (ETFs) are ideal choices because they offer diversifica-tion and professional management. See Chapter 10 for more on mutual funds and ETFs.

Assessing Your Risk-Taking Desires

With money that you're investing for shorter-term goals, you have a more limited menu of investments to choose among. For your emergency/rainy-day fund, for example, you should consider only a money market fund or bank/credit union sav-ings account. Down-payment money for a home purchase that you expect to make in a few years should be kept in short-term bonds.

When you're younger and have more years until you plan to use your money, you should keep larger amounts of your long-term investment money in growth (ownership) invest-ments, such as stocks, real estate, and small business. The attraction of these types of investments is their potential to really grow your money, but the risk is that the value of such investments can fall significantly.

The younger you are, the more time your investments have to recover from a bad fall. A long-held guiding principle says to subtract your age from 110 and invest the resulting number as a percentage of money to place in growth (ownership) investments. So if you're 30 years old:

110 – 30 = 80 percent in growth investments

Should you want to be more conservative, subtract your age from 100:

100 – 30 = 70 percent in growth investments

Want to be even more aggressive? Subtract your age from 120:

120 – 30 = 90 percent in growth investments

These guidelines are general ones that apply to money that you invest for the long term (ideally, for ten years or more).

Chapter 3

Setting Your Return Expectations

* *

In This Chapter

▶ Expected returns from common investments

▶ How returns compound over time

* *

*W*e invest to earn returns. In my experience as a former financial advisor and as a writer interacting with many folks, I still find it noteworthy how many people have unrealistic and inaccurate return expectations for particular investments.

Where do these silly numbers come from? There are numerous sources, most of which have a vested interest in convincing you that you can earn really high returns if you simply buy what they're selling. Examples include newsletter writers, financial advisors, and various financial publishing outlets.

In this chapter, I reveal the actual returns you can reasonably expect from common investments. I also illustrate the power of compounding those returns over the years and decades ahead, and I show you why you won't need superhuman returns to accomplish your personal and financial goals.

Estimating Your Investment's Returns

When examining expected investment returns, you have to be careful because you're largely using historic returns as a guide. Using history to predict the future, especially the near future, is dangerous. History may repeat itself, but not always in exactly the same fashion and not necessarily when you expect it to.

Historical returns should be used only as a guide, not viewed as a guarantee. Please keep that in mind as I discuss the returns on money market funds and savings accounts, bonds, stocks, real estate, and small-business investments in this section.

Money market funds and savings account returns

You need to keep your extra cash that awaits investment (for an emergency) in a safe place, preferably one that doesn't get hammered by the sea of changes in the financial markets. By default and for convenience, many people keep their extra cash in a bank savings account. Banks accounts come with Federal Deposit Insurance Corporation (FDIC) backing, which costs the bank some money. Thus, most banks pay a relatively low interest rate on their savings accounts.

Another place to keep your liquid savings is a money market mutual fund. These funds are the safest types of mutual funds around and, for all intents and purposes, comparable to a bank savings account's safety. Technically, money market mutual funds don't carry FDIC insurance. To date, however, no retail money market fund has lost money for retail shareholders.

The best money market funds generally pay higher yields than most bank savings accounts (although this has been less true in recent years, with low overall interest rates). When shopping for a money fund, be sure to pay close attention to the fund's expense ratio, because lower expenses generally translate into higher yields. If you're in a higher tax bracket, you should also consider tax-free money market funds. (See Chapter 7 for all the details on money market funds.)

If you don't need immediate access to your money, consider using Treasury bills (T-bills) or bank certificates of deposit (CDs), which are usually issued by banks for terms such as 3, 6, or 12 months. The drawback to T-bills and bank certificates of deposit is that you generally incur a transaction fee (with T-bills) or a penalty (with CDs) if you withdraw your investment before the T-bill matures or the CD's term expires. If you can let your money sit for the full term, you can generally earn more in CDs and T-bills than in a bank savings account. Rates vary by bank, however, so be sure to shop around.

Bond returns

When you purchase a bond, you expect to earn a higher yield than you can with a money market or savings account. You're taking more risk because some bond issuers (such as corporations) aren't always able to fully pay back all that they borrow.

By investing in a bond (at least when it's originally issued), you're effectively lending your money to the issuer of that bond (borrower), which is generally the federal government or a corporation, for a specific period of time. Companies can and do go bankrupt, in which case you may lose some or all of your investment. Government debt can go into default as well. Generally, you get paid in the form of a higher yield for taking on more risk when you buy bonds that have a lower credit rating. (See Chapter 9 for more information on bonds, including how to invest in a diversified portfolio of relatively safe bonds.)

Jeremy Siegel, who is a professor of finance at the Wharton School, has tracked the performance of bonds (and stocks) for more than two centuries! His research has found that bond investors generally earn about 4 to 5 percent per year on average.

Returns, of course, fluctuate from year to year and are influenced by inflation (increases in the cost of living). Generally speaking, increases in the rate of inflation, especially when those increases weren't expected, erode bond returns.

Consider a government bond that was issued at an interest rate of 4 percent when inflation was running at just 2 percent. Thus, an investor in that bond was able to enjoy a 2 percent return after inflation, or what's known as the *real return — real* meaning after inflation is subtracted. Now, if inflation jumps to, say, 6 percent per year, why would folks want to buy your crummy 4 percent bond? They wouldn't, unless the price drops enough to raise the effective yield higher.

Longer-term bonds generally yield more than shorter-term bonds, because they're considered to be riskier due to the longer period until they pay back their principal. What are the risks of holding a bond for more years? There's more time for the credit quality of the bond to deteriorate (and for the bond to default), and there's also more time for inflation to come back and erode the purchasing power of the bond.

Stock returns

The long-term returns from stocks that investors have enjoyed, and continue to enjoy, have been remarkably constant from one generation to the next. Since 1802, the U.S. stock market has returned an annual average of about 7 percent per year above the rate of inflation. That's a remarkable track record, but don't forget that it's an annual *average* return.

Stocks have significant downdrafts and can easily drop 10, 20, 30 percent, or more in relatively short periods of time. Stocks can also rise dramatically in value over short periods. The keys to making money in stocks are to be diversified, to invest consistently, and to own stocks over the long run.

Stocks exist worldwide, of course, not just in the United States. When investing in stocks, go global for diversification purposes. International (non-U.S.) stocks don't always move in tandem with U.S. stocks. As a result, overseas stocks help diversify your portfolio. In addition to enabling U.S. investors to diversify, investing overseas has proven to be profitable over the years.

Now, some folks make stock investing riskier than need be by doing some foolish things:

✔ **Chasing after specific stocks or sectors that have recently been hot:** Yes, what a rich genius you'd have been if you'd invested in Apple stock when it went public. With the benefit of hindsight, it's easy to spot the "best" stock investments (companies or sectors) over specific periods. It's quite another thing to put your money on the line now and to hope and expect that you have the ability to pick the best-performing stocks of the future.

✔ **Excessive trading and market timing:** Another type of wishful thinking occurs when folks would like to believe that they can jump into and out of the market at the right times to participate in moves higher and to sidestep downturns.

Chapter 8 goes into detail on stocks, explaining how to invest in them successfully and not lose your shirt.

Is higher economic growth better for stock prices?

Stocks for the Long Run (McGraw-Hill) author Jeremy Siegel makes a surprising statement in his book: "... economic growth has nowhere near as big an impact on stock returns as most investors believe." Siegel presents a long-term analysis going back to 1900, which shows that a country's real GDP growth (that is, growth above the rate of inflation) is negatively correlated with stock market returns.

This surprising finding means that those economies experiencing higher rates of growth actually tend to produce lower long-term stock market returns. Siegel's analysis shows that this fact is even more pronounced in developing countries. China is a recent example of a country that has enjoyed fast rates of growth but relatively low stock market returns.

In explaining how this reality could possibly be, Siegel points out that the primary determinants of stock prices are earnings per-share and dividends per-share. Economic growth doesn't necessarily boost earnings and dividends per-share because growth requires higher capital expenditures, and as Siegel points out, this capital does not come freely. "The added interest costs in the case of debt financing and the dilution of earnings in the case of equity financing reduce the growth of earnings per share," says Siegel.

Real estate returns

Odds are good that you know that in recent years, most types of real estate in most parts of the country have gone down in value. You may think that real estate isn't a good investment, but you'd be wrong.

Real estate is a solid long-term investment. Real estate, as an investment, has produced returns comparable to those of investing in the stock market. Both stocks and real estate have down periods but have historically produced attractive long-term returns.

Real estate does well in the long run because of growth in the economy, in jobs, and in population. Real estate prices in and near major metropolises and suburbs generally appreciate the most because people and businesses tend to cluster in those areas.

I'd like to make an important caution here about viewing a home in which you live solely as an investment. As I discuss in Chapter 11, your primary reason to buy and own a home should not be high expected investment returns, because you won't be earning rental income if you live in your own home. That's why you should thoroughly understand the effect that owning a home will have on your monthly spending and budget. (Investment real estate examples include a small apartment building and retail space.)

Small-business returns

When we think of the "American dream," one of the images that comes to the minds of many folks is owning their own business and possibly making it big by doing so.

You have numerous choices for tapping into the rewards of the small-business world. If you have the drive and determination, you can start your own small business. Or perhaps you have what it takes to buy an existing small business. If you obtain the necessary capital and skills to assess opportunities and risk, you can invest in someone else's small business. None of these avenues is easy. In fact, all these routes require drive, determination, and some skills and money (more on this in Chapter 12).

By starting a small business and retaining a major ownership stake, you can earn very high effective returns. Unlike with the stock market, for which plenty of historic rate-of-return data exists, no specific data exists on the returns that small-time investors have had from investing in small private companies. (We do know that successful venture capital firms, which invest in small businesses with large potential, earn generous returns for the general partners.) Please also note that this investment class, unlike stocks, bonds, and even real estate, doesn't easily allow for diversification if purchased through a real estate investment trust (REIT; see Chapter 11).

While the financial rewards can be attractive, there are other rewards from investing in small businesses. In my small-business ventures, for example, I've enjoyed designing and running businesses that provide useful and valued services. I also enjoy having flexible work hours and not feeling like I'm punching a time clock to satisfy a boss.

Compounding Your Returns

If you've read this chapter up to this point, you see that I've discussed the historic investment returns on common investments. To summarize: During the past century, stocks and investment real estate returned around 9 percent per year, bonds around 5 percent, and savings accounts about 4 percent.

Compounding seemingly modest investment returns can help you accumulate a substantial sum of money to help you accomplish your personal and financial goals.

The value of getting a few extra percent

As I discuss in Chapter 1, the stock market (and real estate) can be risky, which logically raises the question of whether investing in stocks and real estate is worth the anxiety and potential losses. Why bother for a few extra percent per year?

Here's a good answer to that sensible question: Over many years, a few extra percent per year will increase your nest egg dramatically. The more years you have to invest, the greater the difference a few percent makes in your returns (see Table 3-1).

Table 3-1 How Compounding Grows Your Investment Dollars

For Every $1,000 Invested at This Return	In 25 Years	In 40 Years
1%	$1,282	$1,489
2%	$1,641	$2,208
3%	$2,094	$3,262
4%	$2,666	$4,801
5%	$3,386	$7,040
6%	$4,292	$10,286
7%	$5,427	$14,974
8%	$6,848	$21,725
9%	$8,623	$31,409

Here's a practical example to show you what a major difference earning a few extra percent can make in accomplishing your financial goals. Consider a 30-year-old investor who's saving toward retirement on his $40,000 annual salary. Suppose that his goal is to retire by age 67 with about $30,000 per year to live on (in today's dollars), which would be about 75 percent of his working salary.

If he begins saving at age 30, he needs to save about $460 per month if you assume that he earns about 5 percent per year average return on his investments. That's a big chunk to save each year — amounting to about 14 percent of his gross (pretax) salary.

But what if this investor can earn just a few percent more per year on average from his investments — 8 percent instead of just 5 percent? In that case, he could accomplish the same retirement goal by saving just half as much: $230 per month!

Considering your goals

How much do you need or want to earn? You have to balance your goals with how you feel about risk. Some people can't handle higher-risk investments. Although investing in stocks, real estate, or small business can produce high long-term returns, investing in these vehicles comes with greater risk, especially over the short term.

Others are at a time in their lives when they can't afford to take great risk. If you're still in school, if you've lost your job, or if you're starting a family, your portfolio and nerves may not be able to wait a decade for your riskier investments to recover after a major stumble.

If you work for a living, odds are that you need and want to make your investments grow at a healthy clip. Should your investments grow slowly, you may fall short of your goals of owning a home or retiring or changing careers.

All this is to say that you should take the time to contemplate, enumerate, and prioritize your personal and financial goals. If you haven't already sorted them out, see Chapter 2 to get started.

Chapter 4

Minimizing Your Taxes When Investing

*Y*ou must pay attention to tax issues when making investing decisions. Actually, let me rephrase that. Like plenty of other folks, you could ignore or pay half attention to taxes on your investments. Unless you enjoy paying more taxes, however, you should understand and consider tax ramifications when choosing and managing your investments over the years.

Tax considerations alone shouldn't dictate how and where you invest your money. You should also weigh investment choices, your desire and the necessity to take risk, personal likes and dislikes, and the number of years you plan to hold the investment.

In this chapter, I explain how the different components of investment returns are taxed. I also present proven strategies to minimize your investment taxes and maximize your returns. Finally, I discuss tax considerations when selling an investment.

Understanding Investment Taxes

When you invest outside tax-sheltered retirement accounts, the profits and distributions on your money are subject to taxation. (Distributions are taxed in the year that they are paid out; appreciation is taxed only when you sell an investment at a profit.) So the non-retirement-account investments that make sense for you depend (at least partly) on your tax situation.

Tracking taxation of investment distributions

The distributions that various investments pay out and the profits that you may make are often taxable, but in some cases, they're not. It's important to remember that it's not what you make pretax on an investment that matters, but what you get to keep after taxes.

Interest you receive from bank accounts and corporate bonds is generally taxable. U.S. Treasury bonds, which are issued by the U.S. federal government, pay interest that's state-tax-free but federally taxable.

Municipal bonds, which state and local governments issue, pay interest that's federally-tax-free and also state-tax-free to residents in the state where the bond is issued. (For more on bonds, see Chapter 9.)

Taxation on your *capital gains,* which is the profit (sales price minus purchase price) on an investment, is computed under a unique system. Investments held less than one year generate short-term capital gains, which are taxed at your normal marginal income tax rate (which I explain in the next section).

Profits from investments that you hold longer than 12 months are long-term capital gains. Under current tax law, these long-term gains are taxed at a maximum 15 percent rate, except for folks in the two lowest income tax brackets: 10 percent and 15 percent. For these folks, the long-term capital gains tax rate is 0 percent (as in nothing).

Dividends paid out on stock are also taxed at the same favorable long-term capital gains tax rates under current tax law.

If you've been following the activity in Washington in recent years, you may know that these investment tax rates may be changing. As this book goes to press, discussions are under way about a possible increase in the long-term capital gains tax rate and dividend tax rate on higher-income earners.

The Patient Protection and Affordable Care Act (informally referred to as Obamacare) is scheduled in 2013 to increase the tax rate on the net investment income for taxpayers with total taxable income above $200,000 (single return) or $250,000 (joint return). Net investment income includes interest, dividends, and capital gains. The increased tax rate will be 3.8 percent. The outcome of the November 2012 election may affect what happens with the Affordable Care Act and this tax increase.

Determining your tax bracket

Many folks don't realize it, but the federal government (like most state governments) charges you different income tax rates for different parts of your annual income. You pay less tax on the first dollars of your earnings and more tax on the last dollars of your earnings.

Your *federal marginal income tax rate* is the rate of tax that you pay on your last, or so-called highest, dollars of income. Your taxable income is the income that is left after taking allowed deductions on your return.

Your actual marginal tax rate includes state income taxes if your state levies an income tax.

There's value in knowing your marginal tax rate. This knowledge allows you to determine the following (among other things):

- ✔ How much you could reduce your taxes if you contribute more money to retirement accounts
- ✔ How much you would pay in additional taxes on extra income you could earn from working more

✔ How much you could reduce your taxable income if you use investments that produce tax-free income (which might make sense only if you're in a higher tax bracket — more on this later in the chapter).

For the latest federal income tax rates and brackets, please visit my website at www.erictyson.com.

Devising tax-reduction strategies

Use these strategies to reduce the taxes you pay on investments that are exposed to taxation:

✔ **Make use of retirement accounts and health savings accounts.** Most contributions to retirement accounts gain you an immediate tax break, and once they're inside the account, investment returns are sheltered from taxation, generally until withdrawal. See Chapter 2 for details on using retirement accounts when investing.

Similar to retirement accounts are health savings accounts (HSAs). With HSAs, you get a tax break on your contributions up front; investment earnings compound without taxation over time; and there's no tax on withdrawal so long as the money is used to pay for health-related expenses (as delineated by the IRS).

✔ **Consider tax-free money market funds and tax-free bond funds.** Tax-free investments yield less than comparable investments that produce taxable earnings, but because of the tax differences, the earnings from tax-free investments can end up being greater than what taxable investments leave you with. If you're in a high-enough tax bracket, you may find that you come out ahead with tax-free investments.

For a proper comparison, subtract what you'll pay in federal and state taxes from the taxable investment to see which investment nets you more.

✔ **Invest in tax-friendly stock funds.** Mutual funds that tend to trade less tend to produce lower capital gains distributions. For mutual funds held outside tax-sheltered retirement accounts, this reduced trading effectively increases an investor's total rate of return. *Index funds* are mutual funds that invest in a relatively static portfolio of securities, such as stocks and bonds. (This is also true of some exchange-traded funds.) They don't attempt to beat the market; rather, they invest in the securities to mirror or match the performance of an underlying index. Although index funds can't beat the market, the typical actively managed fund doesn't, either, and index funds have several advantages over actively managed funds. See Chapter 10 to find out more about tax-friendly stock mutual funds, including some nonindex funds and exchange-traded funds.

✔ **Invest in small business and real estate.** The growth in value of business and real estate assets isn't taxed until you sell the asset. Even then, with investment real estate, you often can roll over the gain into another property as long as you comply with tax laws. Increases in value in small businesses can qualify for the more favorable longer-term capital gains tax rate and potentially for other tax breaks. However, the current income that small business and real estate assets produce is taxed as ordinary income.

Short-term capital gains (investments held one year or less) are taxed at your ordinary income tax rate. This fact is another reason why you shouldn't trade your investments quickly (within 12 months).

Reducing Your Taxes When Selling Investments

I advocate doing your homework so that you can purchase and hold on to good investments for many years and even decades. That said, each year, folks sell and trade lots of investments.

My experience in helping folks get a handle on their investments suggests that too many people sell for the wrong reasons (while other investors hold on to investments for far too long and should sell them).

In this section, I highlight important tax and other issues to consider when you contemplate selling your investments, but I start with the nontax, bigger-picture considerations.

Weighing nontax issues

Although the focus of this chapter is on tax issues to consider when making, managing, and selling your investments, I'd be remiss not to raise bigger-picture considerations:

- ✔ **Meeting your goals and preferences:** If your life has changed (or if you've inherited investments) since the last time you took a good look at your investment portfolio, you may discover that your current holdings no longer make sense for you. To avoid wasting time and money on investments that aren't good for you, be sure to review your investments at least annually.

Don't make quick decisions about selling. Instead, take your time, and be sure that you understand tax and other ramifications before you sell.

- ✔ **Keeping the right portfolio mix:** A good reason to sell an investment is to allow yourself to better diversify your portfolio. Suppose that through your job, you've accumulated such a hefty chunk of stock in your employer that this stock now overwhelms the rest of your investments. Or perhaps you've simply kept your extra money in a bank account or inherited stock from a dear relative. Conservative investors often keep too much of their money in bank accounts, Treasury bills, and the like. If your situation is like these, it's time for you to diversify. Sell some of the holdings of which you have too much, and invest the proceeds in some of the solid investments that I recommend in this book.

If you think that your employer's stock is going to be a superior investment, holding a big chunk is your gamble. At minimum, review Chapter 8 to see how to evaluate a particular stock. Remember to consider the consequences if you're wrong about your employer's stock. Develop an overall investment strategy that fits your personal financial situation (see Chapter 5).

✔ **Deciding which investments are keepers:** Often, people are tempted to sell an investment for the wrong reasons. One natural tendency is to want to sell investments that have declined in value. Some people fear a further fall, and they don't want to be affiliated with a loser, especially when money is involved. Instead, step back, take some deep breaths, and examine the merits of the investment you're considering selling. If an investment is otherwise still sound, why bail out when prices are down and a sale is going on? What are you going to do with the money? If anything, you should be contemplating buying more of such an investment.

Also, don't make a decision to sell based on your current emotional response, especially to recent news events. If bad news has hit recently, it's already old news. Don't base your investment holdings on such transitory events. Use the criteria in this book for finding good investments to evaluate the worthiness of your current holdings. If an investment is fundamentally sound, don't sell it.

Tuning in to tax considerations

When you sell investments that you hold outside a tax-sheltered retirement account, such as in an IRA or a 401(k), taxes should be one factor in your decision. If the investments are inside retirement accounts, taxes aren't an issue because the accounts are sheltered from taxation until you withdraw funds from them.

Just because you pay tax on a profit from selling a non-retirement-account investment doesn't mean you should avoid selling. With real estate that you buy directly, as opposed to publicly held securities like real estate investment trusts (REITs), you can often avoid paying taxes on the profit that you make. (See Chapter 11 for more information.)

With stocks and mutual funds, you can specify which shares you want to sell. This option makes selling decisions more complicated, but you may want to consider specifying what shares you're selling because you may be able to save taxes. (Read the next section for more information on this option.) If you sell all your shares of a particular security that you own, you don't need to concern yourself with specifying which shares you're selling.

Determining the cost basis of your shares

When you sell a portion of the shares of a security (such as a stock, bond, or mutual fund) that you own, specifying which shares you're selling may benefit you taxwise. Here's an example to show you why you may want to specify selling certain shares — especially those shares that cost you more to buy — so you can save on your taxes.

Suppose that you own 300 shares of a stock, and you want to sell 100 shares. You bought 100 of these shares a long, long time ago at $10 per share, 100 shares two years ago at $16 per share, and the last 100 shares one year ago at $14 per share. Today, the stock is at $20 per share. Although you didn't get rich, you're grateful that you haven't lost your shirt the way some of your stock-picking pals have.

The good tax folks at the Internal Revenue Service allow you to choose which shares you want to sell. Electing to sell the 100 shares that you purchased at the highest price — those you bought for $16 per share two years ago — saves you in taxes. To comply with the tax laws, you must identify the shares that you want the broker to sell by the original date of purchase and/or the cost when you sell the shares. The brokerage firm through which you sell the stock should include this information on the confirmation that you receive for the sale.

The other method of accounting for which shares are sold is the method that the IRS forces you to use if you don't specify before the sale which shares you want to sell — the *first-in-first-out (FIFO) method*. FIFO means that the first shares that you sell are simply the first shares that you bought. Not surprisingly, because most stocks appreciate over time, the FIFO method usually leads to your paying more tax sooner. The FIFO accounting procedure leads to the conclusion that the 100 shares you sell are the 100 that you bought long, long ago at $10 per share. Thus, you owe a larger amount of taxes than if you'd sold the higher-cost shares under the specification method.

Although you save taxes today if you specify selling the shares that you bought more recently at a higher price, when you finally sell the other shares, you'll owe taxes on the larger profit. The longer you expect to hold these other shares, the greater the value you'll likely derive from postponing, realizing the larger gains and paying more in taxes.

When you sell shares in a mutual fund, the IRS has yet another accounting method, known as the *average cost method,* for figuring your taxable profit or loss. This method comes in handy if you bought shares in chunks over time or reinvested the fund payouts in purchasing more shares of the fund. As the name suggests, the average cost method allows you to take an average cost for all the mutual fund shares you bought over time.

Selling large-profit investments

No one likes to pay taxes, of course, but if an investment you own has appreciated in value, someday you'll have to pay taxes on it when you sell. (There is an exception: You hold the investment until your death and will it to your heirs. The IRS wipes out the capital gains tax on appreciated assets at your death.)

Capital gains tax applies when you sell an investment at a higher price than you paid for it. As I explain earlier in this chapter, your capital gains tax rate is different from the tax rate that you pay on ordinary income (such as from employment earnings or interest on bank savings accounts).

Odds are that the longer you've held securities such as stocks, the greater the capital gains you'll have, because stocks tend to appreciate over time. If all your assets have appreciated significantly, you may resist selling to avoid taxes. If you need money for a major purchase, however, sell what you need and pay the tax. Even if you have to pay state as well as federal taxes totaling some 35 percent of the profit, you'll have lots left. (For "longer-term" profits from investments held more than one year, your federal and state capital gains taxes probably would total less than 20 percent to 25 percent.)

Before you sell, do some rough figuring to make sure you'll have enough money left to accomplish what you want. If you seek to sell one investment and reinvest in another, you'll owe tax on the profit unless you're selling and rebuying real estate (see Chapter 11).

If you hold several assets, to diversify and meet your other financial goals, give preference to selling your largest holdings with the smallest capital gains. If you have some securities that have profits and some with losses, you can sell some of each to offset the profits with the losses.

Handling losers in your portfolio

Perhaps you have some losers in your portfolio. If you need to raise cash for some particular reason, you may consider selling select securities at a loss. You can use losses to offset gains as long as you hold both offsetting securities for more than one year (long term) or hold both for no more than one year (short term). The IRS makes this delineation because it taxes long-term gains and losses on a different rate schedule from short-term gains and losses.

If you sell securities at a loss, you can claim up to $3,000 in net losses for the year on your federal income tax return. If you sell securities with net losses totaling more than $3,000 in a year, you must carry the losses over to future tax years. This situation not only creates more tax paperwork, but it also delays realizing the value of deducting a tax loss. Try not to have net losses (losses + gains) that exceed $3,000 in a year.

Some tax advisors advocate doing year-end tax-loss selling with stocks, bonds, and mutual funds. The logic goes that if you hold a security at a loss, you should sell it, take the tax write-off, and then buy it (or something similar) back. When selling investments for tax-loss purposes, be careful of the so-called wash sale rules. The IRS doesn't allow the deduction of a loss for a security sale if you buy that same security back within 30 days. As long as you wait 31 or more days, you won't encounter any problems.

If you're selling a mutual fund or exchange-traded fund, you can purchase a fund similar to the one you're selling to easily sidestep this rule.

Selling investments when you don't know their original cost

Sometimes, you may not know what an investment originally cost you, or you received some investments from another person, and you're not sure what he or she paid for them.

If you don't have the original statement, start by calling the firm where the investment was purchased. Whether it's a brokerage firm or mutual fund company, the company should be able to send you copies of old account statements, although you may have to pay a small fee for this service.

Also, increasing numbers of investment firms, especially mutual fund companies, can tell you upon the sale of an investment what its original cost was. The cost calculated is usually the average cost for the shares you purchased.

Part II
Preparing Your Investing Foundation

The 5th Wave · By Rich Tennant

"Our plan is to pay for the rest of it when we pay off our college loan."

In this part...

I explain important steps you should take before engaging in more serious and potentially rewarding higher-return investments. First up is what should be included in your personal financial plan. Then I discuss using bank and credit union accounts, as well as what they are and aren't good for. Finally, I cover money market funds and how to find the best one for your situation.

Chapter 5

Laying Out Your Financial Plans

In This Chapter

▶ What you should do before investing

▶ How your financial plan translates into your investing plan

*I*nvesting is exciting.

Most folks love to pick an investment, put their money into it, and then enjoy seeing it increase in value. Of course, as I discuss in this book, investing isn't that easy. You can do your homework and make a good decision but then see your well-chosen investment fall in value and test your nerves.

But that's putting the cart before the horse. Before you make any great, wealth-building investments, you should get your financial house in order. Understanding and implementing some simple personal financial management concepts can pay off big for you in the decades ahead.

In this chapter, I explain what financial housekeeping you should do before you invest, as well as how to translate your overall personal and financial plans into an investment plan.

First Priorities: Paying Off High-Cost Debt and Building a Safety Reserve

Plenty of younger folks have debts to pay and lack an emergency reserve of money for unexpected expenses. High-cost debts, such as on a credit card, can be a major impediment to investing, in particular, and accomplishing your future personal and financial goals, in a broader sense. A high interest rate keeps the debt growing and can cause your debt to spiral out of control, which is why I discuss dealing with this debt as your first priority, just before establishing an emergency reserve.

Paying off high-cost consumer debt

Paying down debts isn't nearly as exciting as investing, but it does make your investment decisions less difficult. Rather than spending your time investigating specific investments, paying off your debts with new money you're able to save may indeed be your best investment.

Consumer debt includes borrowing on credit cards, auto loans, and the like, which are often costly ways to borrow. Banks and other lenders charge higher interest rates for consumer debt than for debt for investments, such as real estate and business, because consumer loans are the riskiest type of loans for a lender. Risk means the chance of the borrower's defaulting and being unable to pay back all that he or she borrowed.

Many folks have credit card debt that costs 18 percent or more per year in interest. Some credit cards levy interest rates well above 20 percent if you make a late payment or two. Reducing and eventually eliminating this debt with your savings is like putting your money in an investment with a guaranteed tax-free return equal to the rate that you pay on your debt.

For example, if you have outstanding credit card debt at 18 percent interest, paying off that debt is the same as putting your money to work in an investment with a guaranteed 18 percent tax-free annual return. Because the interest on consumer debt isn't tax-deductible, you would need to earn more than 18 percent by investing your money elsewhere to net

18 percent after paying taxes. Earning such high investing returns is highly unlikely, and to earn those returns, you'd be forced to take great risk.

 Consumer debt is hazardous to your long-term financial health (not to mention damaging to your credit score and future ability to borrow for a home or other wise investments) because it encourages you to borrow against your future earnings. I often hear people say such things as "I can't afford to buy a new car for cash, given how expensive cars are." Well, okay. New cars are expensive, so you need to set your sights lower and buy a good used car that you can afford. You can then invest the money that you'd otherwise spend on your auto loan.

 Now, I do "recommend" one exception to my guideline of not borrowing through a credit card: Tapping credit card debt may make sense if you're financing a business. If you don't have home equity, personal loans (through a credit card or auto loan) may actually be your lowest-cost source of small-business financing (see Chapter 12 for more information).

Establishing an emergency reserve

You never know what life will bring, so having an accessible reserve of cash to meet unexpected expenses makes good financial sense. If you have generous parents or dear relatives, you can certainly consider using them as your emergency reserve. Just be sure that you ask them in advance how they feel about that before you count on receiving funding from them. If you don't have a financially flush family member, the onus is on you to establish a reserve.

 I recommend that you have at least three months' worth of living expenses to as much as six months' worth of living expenses as an emergency reserve. Invest this personal-safety-net money in a money market fund (see Chapter 7). You may also be able to borrow against your employer-based retirement account or against your home equity, should you find yourself in a bind, but these options are much less desirable.

If you don't have a financial safety net, you may be forced, under duress, to sell an investment that you've worked hard for. And selling some investments, such as real estate, can take time and cost significant money (transaction costs, taxes, and so on).

Riskier investments like stocks aren't a suitable place to keep your emergency money invested. While stocks historically have returned about 9 percent per year (see Chapter 3), about one third of the time, stocks decline in value in a given year, sometimes substantially. Stocks can drop and have dropped 20, 30, or 50 percent or more over relatively short periods of time. Suppose that such a decline coincides with an emergency, such as the loss of your job or a health problem that creates major medical bills. Your situation may force you to sell at a loss, perhaps a substantial one. As I discuss in Chapter 5, stocks are intended to be a longer-term investment, not an investment that you expect (or need) to sell in the near future.

What About Paying Down Other Debts?

Getting out from under 18 percent interest rate credit card debt is clearly a priority and a bit of a no-brainer. But what should you do about other debts that carry a more reasonable interest rate? This section talks you through some common examples: student loans and mortgage debt.

Assessing student loans

If you're one of many young adults with lingering student loan debt, you're probably wondering whether you should focus your efforts on paying down that debt or instead invest the extra cash you have.

The best choice hinges upon the interest rate on this debt (after factoring in any tax breaks) and how that compares with the expected return from investing. Of course, you must be reasonable and not pie-in-the-sky about the rate of return you expect from your investments.

Under current tax laws, with student loans, you can deduct up to $2,500 in student loan interest annually on your federal 1040 income tax return. So this deduction can lower the effective interest rate you're paying on your student loans. This deduction is available to single taxpayers with adjusted gross incomes (before subtracting the student loan interest) of $60,000 or less and married couples filing jointly with such incomes of $120,000 or less. Partial deductions are allowed for incomes up to 20 percent above these amounts. Another requirement for taking this deduction is that you and your spouse, if filing jointly, cannot be claimed as dependents on someone else's income tax return.

If you can deduct student loan interest on your tax return, to determine the value of that deduction, please see Chapter 4 to understand what tax bracket you're in (what your marginal tax rate is). For most moderate income earners, 25 percent is a reasonable number to work with.

Suppose that you have student loans outstanding at the attractive interest rate of just 3.5 percent. Assume that you're able to deduct all this interest and that your tax bracket is 25 percent. So after taxes, the effective interest rate on your student loan is 3.5 percent – (0.25 × 3.5 percent) = 2.63 percent.

Now, the question to consider is this: Can you reasonably expect to earn an average annual rate of return from your investments of more than this 2.63 percent? If you invest your money in a sleepy bank account, the answer will probably be no. If you instead invest in things like stocks and bonds, over the long term, you should come out with a higher return.

If you have student loans at a higher interest rate — say, 7.5 percent — it may make more sense to pay those loans down faster with your extra cash than to invest that money elsewhere. To get a higher return than that from investments, you need to take a fair amount of risk, and of course there's no guarantee that you'll actually make a high enough return to make it worth your while.

When deciding whether you should pay down student loans faster, there are some factors to consider besides the cost of your student loans and comparing this cost to the expected return on your investments. Other good reasons not to pay off your student loans any quicker than necessary include the following:

> ✔ **Paying off your student loan faster has no tax benefit.** Instead, you could contribute to your retirement accounts, such as a 401(k), an IRA, or a Keogh plan (especially if your employer offers matching money). Putting additional money in a retirement plan can immediately

reduce your federal and state income tax bills. The more years you have until retirement, the greater the benefit you receive if you invest in your retirement accounts. Thanks to the compounding of your retirement account investments without the drain of taxes, you can actually earn a lower rate of return on your investments than you pay on your student loans and still come out ahead.

✔ **You're willing to invest in growth-oriented, volatile investments, such as stocks and real estate.** To have a reasonable chance of earning more on your investments than it costs you to borrow on your student loans, you must be aggressive with your investments. As I discuss in Chapter 3, stocks and real estate have produced annual average rates of return of about 9 percent. You may be able to earn even more by creating your own small business or by investing in others' businesses.

Keep in mind that you have no guarantee of earning high returns from growth-type investments, which can easily drop 20 percent or more in value over a year or two.

✔ **Paying down your student loans depletes your emergency reserves.** Psychologically, some people feel uncomfortable paying off debt more quickly if it diminishes their savings and investments. You probably don't want to pay down your debt if doing so depletes your financial safety cushion. Make sure that you have access — through a money market fund or other sources (a family member, for example) — to at least three months' worth of living expenses (as I explain in "Establishing an emergency reserve," earlier in this chapter).

Considering paying down mortgage debt

Paying off your mortgage more quickly is an "investment" for your spare cash that may make sense for your financial situation. However, the wisdom of making this financial move isn't as clear as is paying off high-interest consumer debt; mortgage interest rates are generally lower, and the interest is typically tax-deductible.

As with the decision to pay off a student loan faster (review the previous section), when evaluating whether to pay down your mortgage quicker than necessary, you need to compare your mortgage interest rate with your investments' rates of return. Suppose that you have a fixed-rate mortgage with an interest rate of 5 percent. If you decide to make investments instead of paying down your mortgage more quickly, your investments need to produce an average annual rate of return, before taxes, of more than 5 percent for you to come out ahead financially.

Don't get hung up on mortgage tax deductions. Although it's true that mortgage interest is usually tax-deductible, you must also pay taxes on investment profits generated outside retirement accounts. You can purchase tax-free investments like municipal bonds, but over the long haul, such bonds and other types of lending investments (bank savings accounts, CDs, and other bonds) are unlikely to earn a rate of return that's higher than the cost of your mortgage.

Sorting Out Your Financial Plans

I recommend establishing your financial goals before you begin investing. Otherwise, you won't know how much to save or how much risk you need to take or are comfortable taking.

You may want to invest money for several goals, or you may have just one purpose. When I was in my 20s, I put some money away toward retirement, but my bigger priority at that time was to save money so that I could hit the eject button from my management consulting job. I knew that I wanted to start my own business and that in the early years of my entrepreneurial endeavors, I couldn't count on an income as stable or as large as the one I had in consulting.

I invested these two chunks of money quite differently. I kept the money I saved for the start-up of my small business, which was a shorter-term goal, safely invested in a money market fund that had a decent yield but didn't fluctuate in value. By contrast, my retirement was a longer-term goal, so I invested the bulk of my retirement money in stock mutual funds. If these funds fluctuated and declined in value, that was okay in the short term, because I wouldn't be tapping that money.

Considering your investment options and desires

Many good investing choices exist: You can invest in real estate, the stock market, mutual funds, exchange-traded funds, or your own business or someone else's. Or you can pay down debts such as on your student loans, credit cards, auto loan, or mortgage debt more quickly.

What makes sense for you depends on your goals as well as your personal preferences. If you detest risk-taking and volatile investments, paying down some debts, as recommended earlier in this chapter, may make better sense than investing in the stock market.

To determine your general investment desires, think about how you would deal with an investment that plunges 20 percent, 40 percent, or more in a few years or less. Some aggressive investments can fall fast. You shouldn't go into the stock market, real estate, or small business investment arena if such a drop is likely to cause you to sell or make you a miserable wreck. If you haven't tried riskier investments yet, you may want to experiment a bit to see how you feel with your money invested in them.

A simple way to "mask" the risk of volatile investments is to diversify your portfolio — that is, put your money into different investments. Not watching prices too closely helps, too; that's one of the reasons why real estate investors are less likely to bail out when the market declines. Stock market investors, unfortunately from my perspective, can get daily and even minute-by-minute price updates. Add that fact to the quick phone call, click of your computer mouse, or tap on your smartphone that it takes to dump a stock in a flash, and you have all the ingredients for shortsighted investing — and potential financial disaster.

Making investing decisions and determining your likes and dislikes is challenging just when you consider your own concerns. When you have to consider someone else, dealing with these issues becomes doubly hard, given the typically different money personalities and emotions that come into play. In most couples with whom I've worked as a financial counselor, usually one person takes primary responsibility for managing the household finances, including investments. In my observation, the couples that do the best job with their investments are those who communicate well, plan ahead, and compromise.

In my work as a financial counselor, one of the most valuable and difficult things that I did for couples stuck in unproductive patterns of behavior was help them get the issue out on the table. For these couples, the biggest step was making an appointment to discuss their financial management. When they did, I could get them to explain their different points of view and then offer compromises. So be sure to make time to discuss your points of view or hire a financial advisor or psychologist/marriage counselor to help you deal with these issues and differences.

Assessing your savings rate

To accomplish your financial goals, you need to save money, and you also need to know your savings rate. Your savings rate is the percentage of your past year's income that you saved and didn't spend.

Part of being a smart investor involves figuring out how much you need to save to reach your goals. Not knowing what you want to do a decade or more from now is perfectly normal; after all, your goals and needs evolve over the years. But that doesn't mean that you should just throw your hands in the air and not make an effort to see where you stand today and think about where you want to be in the future.

An important benefit of knowing your savings rate is that you can better assess how much risk you need to take to accomplish your goals. Seeing the amount that you need to save to achieve your dreams may encourage you to take more risk with your investments.

During your working years, if you consistently save about 10 percent of your annual income, you're probably saving enough to meet your goals (unless you want to retire at a relatively young age). On average, most people need about 75 percent of their preretirement income throughout retirement to maintain their standards of living.

If you're one of the many people who don't save enough, you need to do some homework. To save more, you need to reduce your spending, increase your income, or both. For most people, reducing spending is the more feasible way to save.

To reduce your spending, first figure out where your money goes. You may have some general idea, but to make changes, you need to have facts. Get out your checkbook register, examine your online bill-paying records, and review your credit card bills and any other documentation that shows your spending history. Tally up how much you spend on dining out, operating your car(s), paying your taxes, and everything else. After you have this information, you can begin to prioritize and make the necessary trade-offs to reduce your spending and increase your savings rate. Earning more income may help boost your savings rate as well. Perhaps you can get a higher-paying job or increase the number of hours that you work. But if you already work a lot, reining in your spending is usually better for your emotional and economic well-being.

If you don't know how to evaluate and reduce your spending or haven't thought about your retirement goals, looked into what you can expect from Social Security, or calculated how much you should save for retirement, now's the time to do so. Pick up the latest edition of my book *Personal Finance For Dummies* (Wiley) to find out all the necessary details for retirement planning and much more.

Investing regularly with dollar cost averaging

Regularly investing money at set time intervals, such as monthly or quarterly, in volatile investments such as stocks, stock mutual funds, or exchange-traded funds is called *dollar cost averaging* (DCA). If you've ever had money regularly deducted from your paycheck and contributed to a retirement savings plan investment account, you've done DCA.

Most folks invest a portion of their employment compensation as they earn it, but if you have extra cash sitting around, you can choose to invest that money in one fell swoop or to invest it gradually via DCA. The biggest appeal of gradually feeding money into the market via DCA is that you don't dump all your money into a potentially overheated investment just before a major drop. No one has a crystal ball and can predict which direction investments will move next in the short term. DCA helps shy investors psychologically ease into riskier investments.

DCA is made to order for skittish investors with larger lump sums of money sitting in safe investments like CDs or savings accounts. It also makes sense for investors with a large chunk of their net worth in cash who want to minimize the risk of transferring that cash to riskier investments, such as stocks.

As with any risk-reducing investment strategy, DCA has its drawbacks. If growth investments appreciate (as they're supposed to), a DCA investor misses out on earning higher returns on his money awaiting investment. Studying U.S. stock market data over seven decades, finance professors Richard E. Williams and Peter W. Bacon found that approximately two thirds of the time, a lump-sum stock market investor earned higher first-year returns than an investor who fed the money in monthly over the first year.

However, knowing that you'll probably be ahead most of the time if you dump a lump sum into the stock market is little solace if you happen to invest just before a major drop in prices. For example, from late 2007 to early 2009, global stocks shed about half of their value.

If you use DCA too quickly, you may not give the market sufficient time for a correction to unfold, during and after which some of the DCA purchases may take place. If you practice DCA over too long a period of time, you may miss a major upswing in stock prices. I suggest using DCA over one to two years to strike a balance.

When you use DCA, establish an automatic investment plan so you're less likely to chicken out. Your money that awaits investment in DCA should have a suitable parking place. I recommend a money market fund that's appropriate for your tax situation.

Knowing the Impact of Investing for College Costs

Many well-intentioned parents want to save for their children's future educational expenses. The mistake that they often make, however, is putting money in accounts in their child's name (in so-called custodial accounts) or saving outside retirement accounts in general. The more money you accumulate outside tax-sheltered retirement accounts, the less assistance you're likely to qualify for from federal and state financial aid sources.

Under the current financial needs analysis used by most colleges in awarding financial aid, the value of your retirement plan is not considered to be an asset. Money that you save outside retirement accounts, including money in the child's name, is counted as an asset and reduces eligibility for financial aid.

Also, be aware that your family's assets, for purposes of financial aid determination, generally include equity in real estate and businesses that you own. Although the federal financial aid analysis no longer counts equity in your primary residence as an asset, many private (independent) schools continue to ask parents for this information when they make their own financial aid determinations. Thus, paying down your home mortgage more quickly instead of funding retirement accounts can harm you financially. You may end up with less financial aid and pay more in taxes.

Make it a priority to contribute to your own retirement savings plan(s). If you instead save money in a nonretirement account for your children's college expenses, you pay higher taxes both on your current income and on the interest and growth of this money. In addition to paying higher taxes, you'll be expected to contribute more to your child's educational expenses because you'll receive less financial aid.

If you're sufficiently wealthy that you expect to pay for your children's full educational costs without applying for financial aid, you can save some on taxes if you invest through custodial accounts. Prior to your child's reaching age 19, the first $1,900 of interest and dividend income is taxed at your child's income tax rate rather than yours. After age 19 (for full-time students, it's those under the age of 24), all income that the investments in your child's name generate is taxed at your child's rate.

Paying for college

If the financial aid system effectively encourages you to save in your own retirement accounts, how will you pay for your kid's education expenses? Here are some ideas and resources:

- ✓ **Home equity:** You can borrow against your home at a relatively low interest rate, and the interest is generally tax-deductible.

- ✓ **Company retirement plans:** 401(k)s, for example, allow borrowing for educational costs.

- ✓ **Student loans:** Several financial aid programs allow you to borrow at reasonable interest rates. The Unsubsidized Stafford Loans and Parent Loans for Undergraduate Students (PLUS), for example, are available, even when your family isn't deemed financially needy.

- ✓ **Grants and scholarships:** Grant programs are available through schools and the government, as well as through independent sources. Complete the Free Application for Federal Student Aid (FAFSA) application to apply for the federal government programs. Grants available through state government programs may require a separate application. Specific colleges and other private organizations — including employers, banks, credit unions, and community groups — also offer grants and scholarships.

- ✓ **Work and save:** Your child can work and save money during high school and college. In fact, if your child qualifies for financial aid, she's generally expected to contribute a certain amount to education costs from employment (both during the school year and summer breaks) and from savings. Besides giving your gangly teen a stake in her own future, this training encourages sound personal financial management down the road.

Paying for college without breaking your budget

One of my favorite financial advice books is Kalman Chany's *Paying For College Without Going Broke* (Random House). Here are some of his top tips, whether you're getting your first degree or going back to school for another one:

✓ **Assume you're eligible.** Don't rule yourself out because of income or academics, and don't rule out a college because you think it's too expensive. The higher the cost, the more aid you may receive.

✓ **Don't wait to be accepted to a college to apply for aid.** The coffers may be empty by spring.

✓ **Get application forms as soon as possible.** You need the federal FAFSA form (http://www.fafsa.ed.gov, 800-433-3243). You may also need to complete the College Board's CSS/PROFILE application, state aid forms, and forms provided by the colleges you're interested in attending.

✓ **Know the deadlines, and be sure to meet each one.** Many colleges have different deadlines for different forms. Some may be due in late December, although most are due in January through March.

✓ **Figure out your expected family contribution.** Before you apply, use worksheets in financial aid guidebooks to calculate what the colleges will estimate you can afford to pay. Be sure to get up-to-date information, as the rules and formulas change every year.

✓ **Maximize your aid eligibility.** Consider also making appropriate adjustments to your assets, debts, and retirement provisions before you apply.

✓ **Follow instructions carefully on the application forms.** Common mistakes that can disqualify your applications are forgetting to sign them, leaving lines blank, or using the wrong academic year's version of the forms.

✓ **Do your income tax forms early.** To meet early aid application deadlines, you may need to do a draft version of your most recent year's income tax return with estimated numbers. Many schools will require a copy of your actual return in the spring to verify your information.

Considering educational savings account options

You'll hear about various accounts you can use to invest money for your kid's future college costs. Tread carefully with these, especially because they can affect future financial aid.

The most popular of these accounts are qualified state tuition plans, also known as Section 529 plans. These plans offer a tax-advantaged way to save and invest more than $100,000 per child toward college costs. (Some states allow upward of $300,000 per student.) After you contribute to one of these state-based accounts, the invested funds grow without taxation. Withdrawals are also tax-free so long as the funds are used to pay for qualifying higher-education costs (which include college, graduate school, and certain additional expenses of special-needs students). The schools need not be in the same state as the state administering the Section 529 plan.

Section 529 plan balances can harm your child's financial aid chances. Thus, such accounts make the most sense for affluent families who are sure that they won't qualify for any type of financial aid. If you do opt for a 529 plan and intend to apply for financial aid, you should be the owner of the accounts (not your child) to maximize qualifying for financial aid.

Investing money earmarked for college

Diversified mutual funds and exchange-traded funds, which invest in stocks in the United States and internationally, as well as bonds, are ideal vehicles to use when you invest money earmarked for college. Be sure to choose funds that fit your tax situation if you invest your funds in nonretirement accounts. (See Chapter 10 for more information.)

When your child is young (preschool age), consider investing up to 80 percent of your investment money in stocks (diversified worldwide) with the remainder in bonds. Doing so can maximize the money's growth potential without taking extraordinary risk. As your child makes his way through the later years of elementary school, you need to begin to make the mix more conservative. Scale back the stock percentage to 50 or 60 percent. Finally, in the years just before the child enters college, reduce the stock portion to no more than 20 percent or so.

Some 529s offer target-date-type funds that reduce the stock exposure as target college dates approach so that you don't have to make the adjustments yourself.

Securing Proper Insurance

As a financial counselor, I've seen that although many people lack particular types of insurance, others possess unnecessary policies. Many people also keep very low deductibles. Remember to insure against potential losses that would be financially catastrophic for you; don't waste your money to protect against smaller losses.

You may be at risk of making a catastrophic investing mistake by not protecting your assets properly. Decisions regarding what amount of insurance you need to carry are, to some extent, a matter of your desire and ability to accept financial risk. But some risks aren't worth taking. Don't overestimate your ability to predict what accidents and other bad luck may befall you.

Here's what insurance I recommend that you have to protect yourself, your loved ones, and your assets:

- ✔ **Major medical health insurance:** You need a policy that pays for all types of major illnesses and major medical expenditures. Consider taking a health plan with a high deductible, which can minimize your premiums. Also consider channeling extra money into a health savings account (HSA), which provides tremendous tax breaks. As with a retirement account, contributions provide an up-front tax break, and money can grow over the years in an HSA without taxation. You can also tap HSA funds without penalty or taxation for a wide range of current health expenses.

- ✔ **Adequate liability insurance on your home and car to guard your assets against lawsuits:** You should have at least enough liability insurance to protect your net worth (assets minus your liabilities/debts) or, ideally, twice your net worth. If you run your own business, get insurance for your business assets if they're substantial. Also consider professional liability insurance to protect against a lawsuit. You may also want to consider incorporating your business. (See Chapter 12 for more on small-business issues.)

✔ **Long-term disability insurance:** Even if you don't have dependents, odds are that you're dependent on your employment income. What would you (and your family) do to replace your income if a major disability prevents you from working? Most large employers offer group plans that have good benefits and are much less expensive than coverage you'd buy on your own. Also check with your professional association for a competitive group plan.

✔ **Life insurance, if others are dependent on your income:** If you're single or your loved ones can live without your income, skip life insurance. If you need coverage, buy term insurance that, like your auto and home insurance, is pure insurance protection. The amount of term insurance you need to buy largely depends on how much of your income you want to replace.

✔ **Estate planning:** Most folks need a simple will to delineate to whom they would like to leave all their worldly possessions. If you hold significant assets outside retirement accounts, you may also benefit from establishing a living trust, which keeps your money from filtering through the hands of probate lawyers. Living wills and medical powers of attorney are useful to have in case you're ever in a medically incapacitated situation. If you have substantial assets, doing more involved estate planning is wise to minimize estate taxes and ensure the orderly passing of your assets to your heirs.

For all the details on the right and wrong ways to buy insurance, what to look for in policies, and where to get good policies, see the latest edition of my book *Personal Finance For Dummies* (Wiley), and visit my website at www.erictyson.com.

Chapter 6

Starting Out with Bank and Credit Union Accounts

* * *

In This Chapter

▶ Understanding what banks are good for and not good for

▶ Evaluating, selecting, and even negotiating with banks

▶ Accessing credit unions and other alternatives to banks

* * *

*C*ustomer visits to stand-alone bank branches with a lobby and tellers are going the way of the big-city-newspaper business. Both are in decline and in industries that are being revolutionized and changed by the Internet.

Who needs retail banks, with their costly-to-maintain branches, when you can do your banking online? You can conduct most transactions quicker online, and it saves the bank money, which enables it to offer you better account terms. And there's no need to rush out at lunchtime to be sure you make it to your bank during its limited open hours. Online banking is generally available 24/7.

But I have even bigger questions for you to consider: Do you even need a bank account, and what are your best alternatives? That's what this chapter explores.

Everyone needs an account or two from which to conduct transactions, including paying bills and storing newly earned money. Such foundational accounts are essential to get in order before proceeding with investing that has the potential to produce higher returns.

Understanding FDIC Bank Insurance

What makes keeping your money in a U.S. bank unique is the Federal Deposit Insurance Corporation (FDIC) insurance that protects bank deposits. If your bank fails (and as history clearly suggests, some banks do fail), and if your bank participates in the FDIC system, your bank account is insured by the U.S. government up to $250,000. The stamp of FDIC backing and insurance is soothing to many folks who worry about all the risks and dangers in the investment world.

While the FDIC insurance is worth something, please remember that banks have to pay for this protection. That cost is effectively passed along to you in the form of lower interest rates on your deposits.

Just because the federal government stands behind the banking FDIC system doesn't mean that your money is 100 percent safe in the event of a bank failure. Although you're insured for $250,000 in a bank, if the bank fails, you may wait quite a while to get your money back — and you may get less interest than you thought you would. Banks fail and will continue to fail. During the 1980s and early 1990s, and again in the late 2000s, hundreds of insured banks and savings and loans failed annually. (Between the early 1990s and mid-2000s — a relatively strong economic period — only a handful of banks failed annually.)

Any investment that involves lending your money to someone else or to some organization, including putting your money in a bank or buying a Treasury bond that the federal government issues, carries risk. Although I'm not a doomsayer, any student of history knows that governments and civilizations fail.

FDIC backing is hardly a unique protection. Every Treasury bond is issued and backed by the federal government, the same debt-laden organization that stands behind the FDIC. Plenty of other nearly equivalent safe lending investments yield higher returns than bank accounts. Highly rated corporate bonds are good examples (see Chapter 9). That's not to say that you shouldn't consider keeping some of your money in a bank. But first, you should be completely aware of the realities and costs of FDIC insurance, which gives many folks somewhat false peace of mind about investing in a bank.

Investing in Banking Account and Savings Vehicles

While traditional banks with walk-in branch locations are shrinking in number due to closures, bank mergers, and failures, online banks are growing — and for good reason. Some of the biggest expenses of operating a traditional retail bank are the cost of the real estate and the related costs of the branch. An online bank eliminates much of those costs; thus, these banks are able, for example, to pay their customers higher interest rates on their account balances. And online banks can offer better terms on checking accounts and loans.

The Internet is lowering costs for many industries, and the banking industry is one of those. This doesn't mean, however, that you should rush out to become a customer of an online bank, because other financial companies, like mutual funds and brokerage firms, offer attractive investment accounts and options as well. (See the section "Exploring Alternatives to Bank Accounts," later in this chapter.)

Bank checking accounts and debit cards

Whether it's paying monthly bills or having something in your wallet to make purchases with at restaurants and retail stores, we all need the ability to conduct transactions and access our money. I'm not a fan of credit cards, because the credit feature enables you to spend money you don't have and carry a debt balance month to month. Notwithstanding the lower short-term interest rates some cards charge to lure new customers, the reality is that borrowing on credit cards is expensive — usually, to the tune of more than 18 percent.

Paying a credit card bill in full each month is the smart way to use such a card and avoid these high interest charges. But about half of all credit card holders use the high-interest-rate credit feature on their cards.

Debit cards are excellent transaction vehicles and a better alternative for folks who are prone to borrow via their credit cards. A debit card connects to your checking account, thus eliminating the need for you to carry around excess cash. And as with a credit card, you can dispute transactions if the product or service isn't what the seller claimed it would be and fails to stand behind it. But unlike a credit card, a debit card has no credit feature, so you can't spend money you don't have. (Some checking accounts offer prearranged lines of credit for overdrafts.)

During periods of low interest rates, the fees levied on a transaction account, like a checking account, should be of greater concern to you than the interest paid on account balances. After all, you shouldn't be keeping lots of extra cash in a checking account; you've got better options for that, which I discuss in the rest of this chapter.

One reason why bank customers have gotten lousy terms on their accounts is that they gravitate toward larger banks and their extensive ATM networks so that they can easily get cash when they need it. These ATM networks (and the often-associated bank branches) are costly for banks to maintain. So you pay higher fees and get lower yields when you're the customer of a bank with a large ATM network, especially a bank that does tons of advertising.

By using a debit card that carries a VISA or MasterCard logo, you won't need to access and carry around much cash. Debit cards are widely accepted by merchants and are connected to your checking account. These cards can be used for purchases and for obtaining cash from your checking account.

Savings accounts and certificates of deposit

Banks generally pay higher interest rates on savings account balances than they do on checking account balances. But they have often lagged behind the best money market funds, offered by mutual fund companies and brokerage firms (see Chapter 7). Online banking is changing that dynamic, however, and now the best banks offer competitive rates on savings accounts.

The virtue of most savings accounts is that you can earn some interest yet have penalty-free access to your money. The investment won't fluctuate in value the way that a bond will, and you don't have early-withdrawal penalties, as you do with a certificate of deposit (CD).

The yield on bank savings accounts is generally pretty crummy. That's why your friendly neighborhood banker will be quick to suggest a CD as a higher-yielding investment alternative to a bank savings account. He or she may tout the fact that unlike a bond (discussed in Chapter 9), a CD doesn't have fluctuating principal value. CDs also give you the peace of mind afforded by the government's FDIC insurance program.

CDs pay higher interest rates than savings accounts because you commit to tie up your money for a period of time, such as 6 or 12 months, or 3 or 5 years. The bank pays you, say, 2 percent and then turns around and lends your money to others through credit cards, auto loans, and so on. The bank charges those borrowers an interest rate of 10 percent or more. Not a bad business!

I'm not a fan of CDs. I've found that investors often use CDs by default without researching their pros and cons. Here are some drawbacks that your banker may neglect to mention:

- ✔ **Early-withdrawal penalties:** When you tie up your money in a CD and later decide that you want it back before the CD matures, a hefty penalty (typically, about six months' interest) is usually shaved from your return. With other lending investments, such as bonds and bond mutual funds, you can access your money without penalty and generally at little or no cost.

- ✔ **Mediocre yields:** In addition to carrying penalties for early withdrawal, a CD yields less than a high-quality bond with a comparable maturity (such as two, five, or ten years). Often, the yield difference is 1 percent or more, especially if you don't shop around and simply buy CDs from the local bank where you keep your checking account.

- ✔ **Only one tax flavor:** High-tax-bracket investors who purchase CDs outside their retirement accounts should be aware of a final and perhaps fatal flaw of CDs: The interest on CDs is fully taxable at the federal and state levels. Bonds, by contrast, are available in tax-free (federal and/ or state) versions, if you desire.

You can earn higher returns and have better access to your money when it's in bonds than you can when it's in CDs. Bonds make especially good sense when you're in a higher tax bracket and would benefit from tax-free income in a nonretirement account. CDs may make sense when you know, for example, that you can invest your money for, say, two years, after which time you need the money for some purchase that you expect to make. Just make sure that you shop around to get the best interest rate from an FDIC-insured bank. If having that U.S. government insurance gives you peace of mind, consider investing in Treasury bonds, which tend to pay more interest than many CDs (see Chapter 9).

Negotiating with Bankers

Especially at traditional bricks-and-mortar banks in your local community, you may be able to get better terms and deals if you ask. Let me give you a common example.

Suppose that for several years, you've had a checking account at your local bank and have not had any real issues or problems. Then one month, you end up bouncing several check payments (say, four at $30 each) because a deposit into your account didn't clear in time. You may very well be able to get some or even all of these fees waived by pleading your case to the local branch manager. Explain how long you've been a good customer and why this was a one-time case of bad luck, something beyond your control, and so on. The worst that can happen is that the manager will turn down your request, and you'll have wasted a few minutes of your day. More likely, however, is that you might save yourself $90 to $120 for a small amount of your time.

Deposit account terms and loan terms are harder to negotiate, but I've seen folks have some success even in those arenas. Your regular bank may offer better mortgage terms if it knows it needs to match or beat a more competitive offer from another bank you've shopped, for example.

Feeling Secure with Your Bank

Putting your money in a bank may make you feel safe for a variety of reasons. For your parents and your grandparents, the first investing experience was likely at the neighborhood bank where they established checking and savings accounts.

Part of your comfort in keeping your money in a bank may stem from the fact that the bank is where your well-intentioned mom and dad may have first steered you financially. Also, at a local branch, often within a short distance of your home or office, you find vaults and security-monitoring cameras to protect your deposits.

Bank branches cost a lot of money to operate. Guess where that money comes from? From bank depositors and the customers of the banks' various services, of course! These operating costs are one of the reasons why the interest rates that banks pay often pale in comparison to some of the similarly secure alternatives discussed elsewhere in this book (such as in Chapter 7, where I discuss money market funds in detail as alternatives to bank savings accounts). This also explains why an online bank may be your best choice if you want to keep some of your money in a bank.

Evaluating any bank

Most folks know to look for a bank that participates in the U.S.-government-operated FDIC program. Otherwise, if the bank fails, your money on deposit isn't protected. FDIC covers your deposits up to a cool $250,000.

Some online banks are able to offer higher interest rates because they are based overseas and, therefore, are not participating in the FDIC program. (Banks must pay insurance premiums into the FDIC fund, which adds, of course, to a bank's costs.) Another risk for you is that noncovered banks may take excessive risks with their business to be able to pay depositors higher interest rates.

When considering doing business with an online bank or a smaller bank you've not heard of, you should be especially careful to ensure that the bank is covered under FDIC. Don't simply accept the bank's word for it or the display of the FDIC logo in its offices or on its website.

Check the FDIC's website database of FDIC-insured institutions to see whether the bank you're considering doing business with is covered. Search by going to the FDIC's Bank Find page (www2.fdic.gov/idasp/main.asp). You can search by the name, city, state, or zip code of the bank. For insured banks, you can see the date when it became insured, its insurance certificate number, the main office location for the bank (and branches), its primary government regulator, and other links to detailed information about the bank. In the event that your bank doesn't appear on the FDIC list, yet the bank claims FDIC coverage, contact the FDIC at (877) 275-3342.

In addition to ensuring that a bank is covered by FDIC, investigate the following:

✓ **What is the bank's reputation for its services?** This may not be easy to discern, but at a minimum, you should conduct an Internet search of the bank's name along with the words *complaints* or *problems* and examine the results.

✓ **How accessible are customer-service people at the bank?** Is a phone number provided on the bank's website? How hard is it to reach a live person? Are the customer-service representatives you reach knowledgeable and service-oriented?

✓ **What are the process and options for getting your money out?** This issue is a good one to discuss with the bank's customer-service people.

✓ **What fees are charged for particular services?** This information should be posted on the bank's website in a section called something like Accounts Terms or Disclosures. Also, request and inspect the bank's Truth in Savings Disclosure, which answers relevant account questions in a standardized format. Figure 6-1 is an example of an online bank's disclosure for savings accounts.

Truth in Savings Disclosure: Savings Account

Minimum balance to open the account — You must deposit $50.00 to open this account.

Rate information — Your interest rate is variable, and the annual percentage yield may be changed at any time at our discretion.

Compounding and crediting frequency — Interest will be compounded every quarter. Interest will be credited to your account every quarter.

Daily balance computation method — We use the daily balance method to calculate the interest on your account. This method applies a daily periodic rate to the principal in the account each day of the statement cycle.

Accrual of interest on noncash deposits — Interest begins to accrue on the first business day after the banking day you deposit noncash items (for example, checks).

Minimum balance to obtain the annual percentage yield disclosed — You must maintain a minimum balance of $15.00 in the account each day of the quarter to obtain the disclosed annual percentage yield.

Transaction limitations — Transfers from an Advantage Savings account to another account or to third parties by preauthorized, automatic, or telephone transfer are limited to six per month, with no transfers by check, draft, debit card, or similar order to third parties.

Minimum balance to avoid imposition of fees — You must maintain a minimum balance of $200.00 each day of the month to avoid monthly maintenance fees.

Fees — A monthly maintenance fee of $3.00 will be imposed if your account balance falls below the daily minimum balance requirement on any day during the month.

May be subject to additional fees for overdrafts or items returned for nonsufficient funds (NSF returned item fee).

Figure 6-1: A sample Truth in Savings Disclosure statement from an online bank.

Protecting yourself when banking online

The attractions of banking online are pretty obvious. For starters, it can be enormously convenient, as you bank when you want on your computer. You don't have to race around during your lunch break to find a local bank branch. And thanks to their lower overhead, the best online banks are able to offer competitive interest rates and account terms to their customers.

You probably know from experience that conducting any type of transaction online is safe as long as you use some common sense and know who you're doing business with before you go forward. That said, others who've gone before you have gotten ripped off, and you do need to protect yourself.

Take the following steps to protect yourself and your identity when conducting business online:

- ✔ Never access your bank accounts from a shared computer or on a shared network, such as the free access networks offered in hotel rooms and in other public or business facilities.

- ✔ Make certain that your computer has antivirus and firewall software that is updated periodically to keep up with the latest threats.

- ✔ Be aware of missed statements, which could indicate that your account has been taken over.

- ✔ Report unauthorized transactions to your bank or credit card company as soon as possible; otherwise, your bank may not stand behind the loss of funds.

- ✔ Use a complicated and unique password (including letters and numbers) for your online bank account.

- ✔ Log out immediately after completing your transactions on financial websites.

Exploring Alternatives to Bank Accounts

If you've been with me since the beginning of this chapter, you know that the best banks that are focused online should have a cost advantage over their peers that have branch locations. Well, there are other financial companies that have similar, and in some cases even better, cost advantages (which translates into better deals for you): credit unions, discount and online brokerage firms, and mutual fund companies.

Credit union accounts and benefits

Credit unions are unique creatures (I guess I should say a unique species) within the financial-services-firm universe. Credit unions are similar to banks in the products and services that they offer (although private banks tend to offer a deeper array). However, unlike banks, which are run as private businesses seeking profits, credit unions operate as non-profit entities and are technically owned by their members (customers).

The best credit unions offer their customers better terms on deposits, including checking and savings accounts (higher interest rates and lower fees) and some loans (lower rates and fees). If they're efficiently operated, they're able to do so because they don't need to make a profit.

Don't assume that credit unions necessarily or always offer better products and services than traditional banks, because they don't. The profit motive of private businesses isn't evil; quite to the contrary, the profit motive spurs businesses to keep getting better at and improving on what they do.

Credit unions have insurance coverage up to $250,000 per customer through the National Credit Union Administration (NCUA), similar to the FDIC protection that banks offer their customers. As when checking out a bank, be sure that any credit union you may deposit money into has NCUA insurance coverage.

The trick to getting access to a credit union is that by law, each individual credit union may offer its services only to a defined membership. Examples of the types of credit union memberships available include

- ✔ Alumni
- ✔ College and university
- ✔ Community
- ✔ Employer
- ✔ Place of worship

There can be some overlap between these groups. To access a credit union, you also may be able to use your family ties.

To find credit unions in your local area, visit the Credit Union National Association website at www.cuna.org, and click the Consumers link.

Brokerage accounts

A type of account worth checking out at brokerage firms is generally known as an asset management account. When these types of accounts first came into existence decades ago, they really were only for affluent investors. That is no longer the case, although the best deals on such accounts at some firms are available to higher-balance investors.

Brokerage firms enable you to buy and sell stocks, bonds, and other securities. Among the larger brokerage firms or investment companies with substantial brokerage operations you may have read or heard about are Charles Schwab, ETrade, Fidelity, ScottTrade, T.D. Ameritrade, and Vanguard.

Now, some of these firms have fairly extensive branch office networks, and others don't. But those that have a reasonable number of branch offices have been able to keep a competitive position because of their extensive customer and asset base and because they aren't burdened by banking regulations (they aren't banks) and the costs associated with operating as a bank.

The best of brokerage firm asset management accounts typically enable you to

- ✔ Invest in various investments, such as stocks, bonds, mutual funds, and exchange-traded funds, and hold those investments in a single account.

- ✔ Write checks against a money market balance that pays competitive yields (although recently, yields have been close to zero).

- ✔ Use a VISA or MasterCard debit card for transactions.

Money market mutual funds

Because bank savings accounts historically have paid pretty crummy interest rates, you need to think long and hard about keeping your spare cash in the bank. Instead of relying on the bank, try keeping your extra savings in a money market fund, which is a type of mutual fund. (Other funds focus on bonds or stocks.) Money market funds historically have offered a higher-yielding alternative to bank savings and bank money market deposit accounts. I use a money market fund that offers unlimited check writing at a mutual fund company. I also don't keep my extra savings in the bank.

The mutual fund business is huge; fund companies hold assets totaling in excess of $12 trillion. A significant portion of that — nearly $3 trillion — is held in money market mutual funds.

A money market fund is similar to a bank savings account except that it is offered by a mutual fund company and therefore lacks FDIC coverage. Historically, this hasn't been a problem, as retail money market funds have never lost shareholder principal for retail investors.

The attraction of money market funds has been that the best ones pay higher yields than bank savings accounts and also come in tax-free versions, which is good for higher-tax-bracket investors. I explain money market funds in greater detail in Chapter 7.

Chapter 7

Managing Money Market Funds

*F*or many years, folks kept their spare cash in a local bank, and for good reason. The local bank was convenient, offered safety and peace of mind with the government backing for money on deposit, and generally paid some interest on the money.

In the 1970s, however, the investment landscape changed for smaller investors. Interest rates and inflation increased, yet banks were limited by regulations in the interest rates they could pay depositors. Thus was born the money market fund.

In this chapter, I discuss the risks and rewards of money funds, uses for funds, and how to pick the best ones to help you meet your investing goals.

Defining Money Market Mutual Funds

Money market mutual funds began in 1971. They invested in the higher-yielding financial instruments that previously were accessible only to larger institutional investors with large sums to invest. Money market funds "democratized" these investments by selling shares to investors with relatively small amounts to invest. By pooling the money of thousands of investors, and after charging a reasonable fee to cover their operational expenses and make a profit, money market funds were able to offer investors a better yield than typical bank accounts.

Money market funds are unique among mutual fund company offerings because they don't fluctuate in value and maintain a fixed $1-per-share price. As with a bank savings account, your principal investment in a money market fund doesn't change in value.

With a money market fund, your investment earns dividends. Dividends are much like the interest you receive from a bank savings account.

Making sense of the appeal of money market funds

The best money market mutual funds offer the following benefits over bank savings accounts:

- **Higher yields:** Money market mutual funds generally yield more because they don't have the higher costs that banks do from having branch offices all over. Banks can get away with paying lower yields because they know that many depositors believe that the Federal Deposit Insurance Corporation (FDIC) insurance that comes with a bank savings account makes it safer than a money market mutual fund. (For more on the safety of money funds compared with banks, see the next section, "Understanding the drawbacks of money market funds"). Also, the FDIC insurance is an expense that banks ultimately pass on to their customers. (See Chapter 6 for more on banks and banking options.)

- **Tax-free flavors:** If you're in a high tax bracket, tax-free money market funds offer you something that bank accounts don't. Bank accounts only pay interest that is fully taxable at both the federal and state levels. Money market funds can be state and federal tax-free (for folks in high tax brackets), just federal tax-free (for folks in a high federal tax bracket), or fully taxable.

✔ **Check writing:** Another useful feature of money market mutual funds is the ability they provide you to write checks, free of charge, against your account. Most mutual fund companies require that the checks that you write be for larger amounts—typically $250 minimum. Some brokerage cash management accounts that include money funds (at firms like Charles Schwab, Fidelity, T.D. Ameritrade, and Vanguard) allow you to write checks for any amount. With these types of money market fund accounts, you can ditch your bank completely because such accounts often come with debit cards that you can use at bank ATMs for a nominal fee. (Some brokerage firms levy service fees if you don't have enough assets with them or don't have regular monthly electronic transfers, such as direct deposit of your paycheck.)

Understanding the drawbacks of money market funds

The best money market mutual funds have higher yields, tax-free alternatives, and check writing — features not offered by bank savings accounts. But you need to know about one difference between bank accounts and money market mutual funds: Money funds aren't insured (except for a one-year period during the 2008–2009 financial crisis).

Bank accounts come with FDIC insurance that protects your deposited money up to $250,000 (see Chapter 6). So if a bank fails because it lends too much money to people and companies that go bankrupt or abscond with the funds, you should get your money back from the FDIC.

The lack of FDIC insurance on a money fund shouldn't trouble you, however. Mutual fund companies can't fail because they have a dollar invested in securities for every dollar that you deposit in their money funds. By contrast, banks are required to have available just a portion — about 10 cents for every dollar that you hand over to them.

Cases have occurred in which money market funds bought some bad investments. However, in all cases involving funds taking in money from retail investors like you and me, the money funds always kept their $1-per-share price.

If you're concerned about the lack of FDIC insurance on a money market fund, stick with bigger mutual fund companies. They have the financial wherewithal and the biggest incentive to save a foundering money fund. Fortunately, the bigger fund companies have the best money funds anyway.

Understanding Money Market Fund Holdings

Money market funds are a safe, higher-yielding alternative to bank accounts. Under Securities and Exchange Commission regulations, money market funds can invest only in the highest-credit-rated securities, and their investments must have an average maturity of less than 60 days. The short-term nature of these securities effectively eliminates the risk of money market funds being sensitive to changes in interest rates (a concern with bonds, which are covered in Chapter 9).

The securities that money market funds buy and hold are extremely safe. General-purpose money market funds invest in government-backed securities, bank certificates of deposit, and short-term corporate debt that the largest and most cred-itworthy companies and the U.S. government issue.

You may not know (or care) what these holdings are. However, here's a short explanation of the most common money fund holdings to aid your understanding and comfort level:

- ✓ **Commercial paper:** Larger corporations often need to borrow money to help make their businesses grow and prosper. In the past, most companies needing a short-term loan had to borrow money from a bank. In recent decades, issuing short-term debt known as *commercial paper* directly to interested investors has become easier. Money market funds buy high-quality commercial paper issued by large companies, banks, and foreign governments.

- ✓ **Certificates of deposit:** When you put your money in a certificate of deposit (CD) at your local bank, what you're doing is making a specific-term loan (3 months, 6 months, 2 years) to your bank. Money market funds can buy CDs as well. When they do, however, they usually invest millions of dollars in bank CDs. Thus, they can command a higher interest rate than you can get on your own. Money funds buy CDs that mature within a couple of months. The money fund is insured only up to $250,000 per bank CD (so they may use multiple banks), just like the bank insurance that customers receive. As with other money fund investments, the money fund does research to determine the credit quality of banks and other institutions that it invests in. Remember that money funds' other investments aren't insured.

✔ **Government debt:** The U.S. federal government has trillions of dollars in debt outstanding in the form of Treasury securities. In addition to investing in Treasuries soon to mature, money funds invest in short-term debt issued by government-affiliated agencies. Some money market funds specialize in certain types of government securities that distribute tax-free income to their investors. Treasury money market funds, for example, buy Treasuries and pay dividends that are state-tax-free but federally taxable. State-specific municipal money market funds invest in debt issued by state and local governments in one state. The dividends on state money funds are federal-tax-free and state-tax-free, if you're a resident of that state.

Protecting and Accessing Your Money in Money Funds

A potentially big psychological impediment to some folks using money funds is that they must deal with money funds online, by phone, and through the mail. That creates some worries, like one of your checks getting lost or stolen and how accessible your money will be for you, but protecting and accessing your money isn't as challenging as it may seem.

Protecting your money

Checks received and sent from a money market fund are just as safe as those received and sent from any other type of account. No one can legally cash a check made payable to you. Don't mistakenly think that going to your local bank in person is safer. Bank robberies happen all the time, totaling more than 5,000 annually.

If you're really concerned about the mail, use a fund company or discount broker with branch offices reasonably close to your home or office. I don't recommend spending the extra money and time required to send your check by way of registered or certified mail. You know if your check got there when you get the statement from the fund company processing the deposit.

In those rare cases where a check does get lost, remember that checks can be reissued. And when you're depositing a check made payable to you, be sure to endorse the check with the notation "For deposit only" along with your account number under your signature. Increasing numbers of banks and credit unions are offering the ability to deposit your checks electronically after you take a picture of it with your smart phone.

Accessing your money

With most money market mutual funds, you will likely be sending your money to a company out of state, so it may seem to you that you won't be able to access these funds efficiently if you needed to. However, you can efficiently tap your money market fund in a variety of ways. You can use the following methods at most fund companies:

- ✔ **Check writing:** The simplest way to access your money market fund is to write a check. Suppose that you have an unexpectedly large expense that you can't afford to pay out of your bank checking account. Just write a check on your money market mutual fund.

- ✔ **Electronic transfers:** Another handy way to access your money is to call the fund company and ask to have money sent electronically from your money market fund to your bank account, or vice versa. Such transactions can also usually be done on fund companies' websites. Or you can have the fund company mail you a check for your desired amount from your money fund (although that obviously isn't a "quick" way to get needed money). If you need money regularly sent from your money market fund to, say, your local bank checking account, you can set up an automatic withdrawal plan. On a designated day of the month, your money market fund electronically sends money to your checking account.

✔ **Debit cards:** Brokerage account money funds that offer debit cards allow access to your money through bank ATMs. Just find out first what fees you may have to pay for using particular ATM networks.

✔ **Wiring:** If you need cash in a flash, many money market funds offer the option of wiring money to and from your bank. Both the money market fund and the bank usually assess a small charge for this service. Most companies can also send you money via an overnight express carrier, such as Federal Express, if you provide an account number.

Unlike when you visit a bank, you can't simply drop by the branch office of a mutual fund company (even if it happens to be nearby) and withdraw funds from your account. Money market fund companies don't keep money in branch offices because they're not banks. However, you can establish the preceding account features, if you didn't set them up when you originally set up your account, by mailing in a form or by visiting the fund's branch office.

Using Money Market Funds in Your Investment Plan

The best money market funds enable you to substitute for a bank savings account while offering comparable safety to a bank, but with a better yield. Money market funds are well suited for some of the following purposes:

✔ **Rainy-day/emergency reserve:** Because you don't know what the future holds, you're wise to prepare for the unexpected, such as job loss, the desire to take some extra time when changing jobs, unexpected health care bills, or a leaky roof on your home. Three to six months' worth of living expenses is a good emergency reserve target for most people. (If you spend $2,500 in an average month, for example, keep $7,500 to $15,000 in reserve.) Three months' living expenses may do if you have other accounts, such as a 401(k), or family that you could tap for a loan. Keep up to one year's expenses if your income fluctuates greatly. If your profession involves a high risk of job loss, and if finding another job could take a long time, you also need a significant cash safety net.

✔ **Short-term savings goals:** If you're saving money for
a big-ticket item that you hope to purchase within the
next couple of years — whether it's a high-def television,
car, or a down payment on a home — a money market
fund is a sensible place to save the money. With a short
time horizon, you can't afford to expose your money to
the gyrations of stocks or longer-term bonds. A money
market fund offers a safe haven for your principal and
some positive return.

✔ **A parking spot for money awaiting investment:** Suppose
you have a chunk of money that you want to invest for
longer-term purposes, but you don't want to invest it
all at once, for fear that you may buy into stocks and
bonds just before a big drop. A money market fund can
be a friendly home to the money awaiting investment as
you gradually move it into your chosen investment. (I
explain this technique, known as dollar cost averaging, in
Chapter 5.)

✔ **Personal checking accounts:** You can use money market
funds with no restrictions on check writing for household
checking purposes. Some discount brokerage services
that offer accounts with a check-writing option downplay
the fact that an investor is allowed to write an unlimited
number of checks in any amounts on his or her account.
You can leave your bank altogether; some money funds
even come with debit cards that you can use at bank
ATMs for a nominal fee.

✔ **Business accounts:** You can also open a money market
fund for your business. You can use this account for
depositing checks received from customers and holding
excess funds, as well as for paying bills by means of the
check-writing feature. Some money funds allow checks to
be written for any amount, and such accounts can completely replace a bank checking account.

Shopping for the Best Money Funds

If you're interested in putting some of your money into a
money market mutual fund, in this section, I name names.
Before getting to that however, allow me to explain what I
look for when selecting a money market fund.

Understanding traits of leading money funds

When looking for an outstanding money market fund, look for these attributes:

✔ **Low expenses:** Select a money market fund that does a good job of controlling its expenses. The operating expenses that the fund deducts before payment of dividends are the biggest determinant of yield. All other things being equal (which they usually are with different money market funds), lower operating expenses translate into higher yields for you. Within a given category of money market funds (general, Treasury, municipal, and so on), fund managers invest in the same basic securities. The market for these securities is pretty darn efficient, so "superstar" money market fund managers may eke out an extra 0.1 percent per year in yield, but not much more. Lower expenses don't mean that a fund company cuts corners or provides poor service. By attracting more money to manage, larger funds are able to manage money for a lower expense percentage.

✔ **Tax appropriate for your situation:** With money market funds, all your return comes from dividends. What you actually get to keep of these returns is what's left over after the federal and state governments take their cut of your investment income. If you invest money that's held outside a retirement account, and you're in a high tax bracket, you may come out ahead if you invest in tax-free money market funds. (*Tax-free* refers to the taxability of the dividends that the fund pays. You don't get a tax deduction for money that you put into the fund, as you do with certain retirement accounts.) If you're in a high-tax state, a state money market fund — if a good one exists for your state — may be a sound move.

✔ **Other attractive fund offerings:** Consider what other investing you plan to do at the fund company where you establish a money market fund. Suppose that you decide to make mutual fund investments in stocks and bonds at a specific fund company. In that case, keeping a money market fund at a different firm that offers a slightly higher yield may not be worth the time and administrative hassle, especially if you don't plan on holding much cash in your money market fund.

✓ **Associated services:** Good money market funds offer other useful services, such as free check writing, telephone exchange and redemptions, and automated electronic exchange services with your bank account.

Most mutual fund companies don't have many local branch offices. Generally, this fact helps fund companies keep their expenses low so they can pay you greater money market fund yields.

You may open and maintain your mutual fund account via the fund's toll-free phone lines, the mail, or the company's website. You don't really get much benefit from selecting a fund company with an office in your area (although you may feel some peace of mind).

Naming good money funds

Using the criteria in the preceding section, in this section, I recommend good money market funds — that is, those that offer competitive yields, check writing, access to other excellent mutual funds, and other commonly needed money market services.

Money market funds that pay taxable dividends may be appropriate for retirement account funds that await investment as well as non-retirement-account money when you're not in a high federal tax bracket and aren't in a high state tax bracket (less than 5 percent).

Here are the best taxable money market funds to consider:

✓ Fidelity Cash Reserves

✓ T. Rowe Price Summit Cash Reserves (higher yields if you invest $25,000)

✓ Vanguard's Prime Money Market

Consider U.S. Treasury money market funds if you prefer a money market fund that invests in U.S. Treasuries, which maintain the safety of government backing, or if you're not in a high federal tax bracket but are in a high state tax bracket (5 percent or higher).

Here are the U.S. Treasury funds that I recommend:

✔ Fidelity's Government Money Market ($25,000 minimum)

✔ USAA's Treasury Money Market

✔ Vanguard Admiral Treasury Money Market

Municipal (also known as *muni*) money market funds invest in short-term debt that state and local governments issue. A municipal money market fund, which pays you federally tax-free dividends, invests in munis issued by state and local governments throughout the country.

A state-specific municipal fund invests in state and local government-issued munis for one state, such as New York. So if you live in New York and buy a New York municipal fund, the dividends on that fund are federal and New York state tax-free.

So how do you decide whether to buy a nationwide or state-specific municipal money market fund? Federal tax-free-only money market funds may be appropriate when you're in a high federal tax bracket but not in a high state bracket (less than 5 percent). State tax-free municipal money market funds are worth considering when you're in a high federal and a high state tax bracket (5 percent or higher).

If you're in a higher state tax bracket, your state may not have good (or any) state tax-free municipal money market funds available. If you live in any of those states, you're likely best off with one of the following national municipal money market funds:

✔ T. Rowe Price Summit Municipal Money Market ($25,000 minimum)

✔ USAA Tax-Exempt Money Market

✔ Vanguard Tax-Exempt Money Market

Fidelity, USAA, and Vanguard have good funds for several states. If you can't find a good state-specific fund for your state, or you're in a high federal tax bracket only, use one of these nationwide muni money markets.

Alternatives to Money Market Mutual Funds

Banks have developed an account that is similar to a money market mutual fund, which they typically call a money market deposit account (MMDA). Banks set the interest rate on MMDAs, and historically, those rates have been a bit lower than what you can get from one of the better money market mutual funds (although this has been less true during the extended period of low interest rates in the early 2010s). Check writing on MMDAs, if it's available, may be restricted to a few checks monthly.

As latecomers to the mutual fund business, some banks now offer real money market mutual funds, including tax-free money funds. Again, the better money market mutual funds from mutual fund companies are generally superior to those offered by banks. The reason: Most bank money market funds have higher operating expenses and, hence, lower yields than the best money funds offered by mutual fund companies.

Although I advocate use of the best money market funds, I realize that a bank or credit union savings account is sometimes the most practical place to keep your money. Your local bank, for example, may appeal to you if you like being able to conduct business face to face. Perhaps you operate a business where a lot of cash is processed; in this case, you probably can't beat the convenience and other services that a local bank offers.

If you have only $1,000 or $2,000 to invest, a bank savings account may be your better option; the best money market funds generally require a higher minimum initial investment.

For investing short-term excess cash, you may first want to consider keeping it in your checking account. This option may make financial sense if the extra money helps you avoid monthly service charges because your balance occasionally dips below the minimum. In fact, keeping money in a separate savings account rather than in your checking account may not benefit you if service charges wipe out your interest earnings. This is especially true with interest rates at such relatively low levels.

Be sure to shop around for the best deals on your checking account because minimum balance requirements, service fees, and interest rates vary. Credit unions offer some of the best deals, although they usually don't offer extensive access to free ATMs (see Chapter 6). The largest banks with the most ATM machines generally have the worst terms on checking and savings accounts.

Part III
Beginning Investments

The 5th Wave   By Rich Tennant

"My plan is to build a diversified portfolio of stocks, money-market investments, and short-term bonds, contribute to a retirement account; and build capital toward a down payment on a house. Or, I'll buy a Corvette."

In this part...

1 delve into the core investments that can do the heavy lifting and hard work for your portfolio in the long haul. I start with explaining stocks and bonds and how to make money with them. I also discuss how to use funds — mutual funds and exchange-traded funds — to invest in stocks, bonds, and other common investments.

Chapter 8

Getting Your Slice of Capitalism with Stocks

● ●

In This Chapter

▶ Understanding what a stock is

▶ Making money in stocks

▶ Choosing among stock buying methods

● ●

*I*s it true that only the rich get richer and that to get ahead, you have to know the right people?

I've never been a fan of the class warfare that too often permeates our political discourse. One reason for my distaste is the simple fact that the facts are on the side of capitalism's being the best system to allow folks of all different means to better their lives and enjoy a good standard of living.

Consider the opportunity to share in the upside presented by owning a stake in successful businesses. That's exactly what you're doing when you buy shares of stock, either through funds or directly through a stock exchange.

You don't need big bucks or the right connections or inside information to earn handsome long-term returns in stocks. (Trading on true inside information can land you in legal hot water.) You simply need to read and digest the time-tested principles I present in this chapter.

I explain what stocks are, how you can make money with them, and the pros and cons of the various methods for purchasing them. I also detail how to time your purchases and sales, and how to sidestep disasters and maximize your chances for success.

What Are Stocks?

Entrepreneurs start companies, and at some point in that process, perhaps even many years after the company was initially formed, company founders may sell shares of owner-ship in the company known as *stock*. Some companies choose to issue stock to raise money, whereas others choose to issue bonds, which are simply loans that the company promises to repay (see Chapter 9).

When you and other members of the investing public buy stock, these outside investors continue to hold and trade it over time. From time to time, some companies may choose to buy some of their own stock back, usually because they think it's a good investment, but they're under no obligation to do so.

By issuing stock, company founders and employee–owners are able to sell some of their relatively illiquid private stock and reap the rewards of their successful company. Growing companies also generally favor stock offerings (over selling bonds to investors) because the company doesn't want the future cash drain that comes from paying loans (bonds) back.

Although many company owners like to take their companies public (issuing stock) to cash in on their stake in the com-pany, not all owners want to go public, and not all who do go public are happy that they did. One of the numerous draw-backs of establishing your company as public includes the burdensome financial reporting requirements, such as pub-lishing quarterly earnings statements and annual reports.

Regulatory required documents not only take lots of time and money to produce, but they can also reveal competitive secrets. Some companies also harm their long-term planning ability because of the pressure and focus on short-term cor-porate performance that comes with being a public company.

From your perspective as a potential investor, you can usually make more money in stocks than bonds, but stocks are gener-ally more volatile in the short term. You can also get burned when buying stock when a company is issuing new stock for the first time, through what is called an *initial public offering* (IPO).

Ultimately, companies seek to raise capital in the lowest-cost way they can, so they elect to sell stocks or bonds based on what the finance folks tell them is the best option. For example, if the stock market is booming and new stock can sell at a premium price, companies opt to sell more stock through an IPO.

You generally should avoid IPOs, because newly issued stock more often than not declines or underperforms in price soon after the offering. (The 2012 Facebook offering is a well-known example, with the stock dropping by more than half in just the first few months after its debut.) Some companies prefer to avoid debt because they don't like carrying it.

When a company decides to issue stock, the company's management team works with investment bankers, who help companies decide when and at what price to sell stock. When a company issues stock, the price per share that the stock is sold for is somewhat arbitrary.

The amount that a prospective investor will pay for a particular portion of the company's stock should depend on the company's profits and future growth prospects. Companies that produce higher levels of profits and grow faster generally command a higher sales price for a given portion of the company.

 A stock's price per share by itself is meaningless in evaluating whether to buy a stock. Ultimately, the amount that investors will pay for a company's stock should depend greatly on the company's growth and profitability prospects, which I discuss in the next section.

How (And Why) You Can Make Money with Stocks

Understanding why stocks tend to appreciate over time and produce better returns than bonds and bank accounts is really pretty simple. In this section, I explain how corporate profits drive stock prices and the different ways you can make money from stocks.

Understanding the importance of corporate profits

The goal of most companies is to make a profit, or earnings. *Earnings* result from the difference between what a company takes in (revenue) and what it spends (costs). I say *most companies* because some organizations' primary purpose is not to maximize profits.

Nonprofit organizations — such as the American Cancer Society, Goodwill, Red Cross, and numerous medical centers, colleges, and universities — are well-known examples. However, I must note that even nonprofits can't thrive and prosper over the long haul without a steady flow of money.

Companies that trade publicly on the stock exchanges seek to maximize their profit; that's what their shareholders want. Higher profits generally make stock prices increase. Most private companies seek to maximize their profits as well, but they retain much more latitude to pursue other goals.

Among the major ways that successful companies increase profits are

- **Building (or buying) a brand name:** What comes to mind when you think of Apple, Cheesecake Factory, Chipotle, Google, McDonald's, Panera Bread, UPS, Verizon Wireless, and Walmart? These are all powerful brand names that have taken their respective companies many years and many dollars to build. Companies with recognizable and positive brand images enjoy more consumer traffic, sales, and profits.

- **Containing costs:** Well-managed companies continually search for ways to control costs. Lowering the cost of manufacturing their products or providing their services allows companies to offer their products and services at lower prices. Managing costs may help boost a company's profits. The marketplace and a company's reputation (and the threat of lawsuits) keep companies from cutting corners and making their products and services dangerous in some way.

- **Developing superior products or services:** Some companies develop or promote an invention or innovation that better meets customer needs. For example, just about every product that Apple has developed, like the iPad, fits that description.

✔ **Monitoring competitors:** Successful companies don't follow the herd, but they do keep an eye on what their competition is up to. If lots of competitors target one part of the market, some companies target a less-pursued segment that, if they can capture it, may produce higher profits thanks to reduced competition.

✔ **Selling products and services in new markets:** Many successful U.S.-based companies, for example, have been expanding into foreign countries to sell their products. Although some product or service adaptation is generally required to sell overseas, selling a proven, developed product or service to new markets generally increases a company's chances for success.

Making sense of how you profit with stocks

Company stock prices tend to rise over time as the company's profits increase. So how do you make money investing in the company's stock? When you purchase a share of a company's stock, you can profit from your ownership in two ways:

✔ **Price appreciation:** When the price per share of your stock rises to a higher price than you originally paid for it, you can make money. This profit, however, is only on paper until you sell the stock, at which time you realize a capital gain. Such gains realized over periods longer than one year are taxed at the lower long-term capital gains tax rate (see Chapter 4). Of course, the stock price per share can fall below what you originally paid, in which case you have a loss on paper unless you realize that loss by selling at a lower price than you paid for the stock.

✔ **Dividends:** Most stocks pay dividends. Companies generally make some profits during the year. Some high-growth companies reinvest most or all of their profits right back into the business. Many companies, however, pay out some of their profits to shareholders in the form of dividends.

Your total return from investing in a stock, then, comes from dividends and appreciation. Stocks differ in the dimensions of these possible returns, particularly with respect to dividends. (See the sections on stock funds and exchange-traded funds in Chapter 10 for more information.)

Timing Your Stock Buying and Selling

One of the biggest temptations and one of the mistakes you're most likely to make investing in stocks is trying to jump into and out of stocks based on your shorter-term expectations of where a particular stock or the market as a whole may be heading.

In this section, I explain what the major market indexes mean and what value there may be in "following" any of them. I cover what measures might be useful in spotting when to buy and sell, and what problematic practices are likely to undermine your stock market investing success.

Following market indexes

You invest in stocks to share in the rewards of capitalistic economies. When you invest in stocks, you do so through the stock market. When people talk about "the market," they're usually referring to the Dow Jones Industrial Average (DJIA), a widely watched U.S. stock market index created by Charles Dow and Eddie Jones of *The Wall Street Journal*. The DJIA market index tracks the performance of 30 large companies that are headquartered in the United States, but it's not the only index.

Indexes serve the following purposes:

✔ They can quickly give you an idea of how particular types of stocks fare and perform in comparison with other types of stocks.

✔ They enable you to compare or benchmark the performance of your stock market investments. If you invest primarily in large-company U.S. stocks, for example, you should compare the overall return of the stocks in your portfolio to a comparable index — in this case, the S&P 500 (which I define later in this chapter).

You may also hear about some other types of more narrowly focused indexes, including those that track the performance of stocks in particular industries, such as advertising, banking, computers, pharmaceuticals, restaurants, semiconductors, textiles, and utilities. Other indexes cover other stock markets, such as those in the United Kingdom, Germany, France, Canada, and Hong Kong.

Focusing your investments on the stocks of just one or two industries or smaller countries is dangerous due to the lack of diversification and your lack of expertise in making the difficult decision about what to invest in and when. Thus, I suggest that you ignore these narrower indexes.

In addition to the DJIA, important market indexes and the types of stocks they track include

- **Standard & Poor's (S&P) 500:** Like the DJIA, the S&P 500 tracks the price of 500 larger-company U.S. stocks. These 500 big companies account for more than 75 percent of the total market value of the tens of thousands of stocks traded in the United States. Thus, the S&P 500 is a much broader and more representative index of the larger-company stocks in the United States than is the DJIA.

- **Russell 2000:** This index tracks the market value of 2,000 smaller U.S. company stocks of various industries. Although small-company stocks tend to move in tandem with larger-company stocks over the longer term, it's not unusual for one to rise or fall more than the other or for one index to fall while the other rises in a given year.

- **Wilshire 5000:** Despite its name, the Wilshire 5000 index actually tracks the prices of about 4,000 stocks of U.S. companies of all sizes — small, medium, and large. Thus, many people consider this index to be the broadest and most representative of the overall U.S. stock market.

- **MSCI EAFE:** Stocks don't exist only in the United States. MSCI's EAFE (Europe, Australasia, and Far East) index tracks the prices of stocks in the other major developed countries of the world.

✔ **MSCI Emerging Markets:** This index follows the value of stocks in less economically developed but emerging countries, such as South Korea, Brazil, China, Russia, Taiwan, India, South Africa, and Mexico. These stock markets tend to be more volatile than those in established economies. During good economic times, emerging markets usually reward investors with higher returns, but stocks can fall farther and faster than stocks in developed markets.

Using price/earnings ratios to value stocks

The level of a company's stock price relative to its earnings or profits per share helps you measure how expensively, cheaply, or fairly a stock price is valued.

Over the long term, stock prices and corporate profits tend to move in tandem. The *price/earnings (P/E) ratio* compares the level of stock prices to the level of corporate profits, giving you a good sense of the stock's value. Over shorter periods of time, investors' emotions as well as fundamentals move stocks, but over longer terms, fundamentals possess a far greater influence on stock prices.

P/E ratios can be calculated for individual stocks as well as entire stock indexes, portfolios, or funds. The P/E ratio of U.S. stocks has averaged around 15 over the past century. During times of low inflation, the ratio has tended to be higher — in the high teens to low twenties.

Just because U.S. stocks have historically averaged P/E ratios of about 15 doesn't mean that every individual stock will trade at that P/E level. Faster-growing companies usually command higher P/E ratios.

Just because a stock price or an entire stock market seems to be at a high price level doesn't necessarily mean that the stock or market is overpriced. Compare the price of a stock to that company's profits per share or the overall market's price level to the overall corporate profits. The P/E ratio captures this comparison. Faster-growing and more-profitable companies generally have higher P/E ratios (meaning that they sell for a premium). Also remember that future earnings, which are difficult to predict, influence stock prices more than current earnings, which are old news.

Most of the time, the stock market is reasonably efficient. By that, I mean that a company's stock price normally reflects many smart people's assessments as to what is a fair price. Thus, it's not realistic for an investor to expect to discover a system for how to "buy low and sell high." Some professional investors may have some ability to spot good times to buy and sell particular stocks, but doing so consistently is enormously difficult.

The simplest and best way to make money in the stock market is to consistently and regularly feed new money into building a diversified and larger portfolio. If the market drops, you can use your new investment dollars to buy more shares. The danger of trying to time the market is that you may be out of the market when it appreciates greatly and in the market when it plummets.

Avoiding temptations and hype

Because the financial markets move on the financial realities of the economy and companies, as well as on people's expectations and emotions (particularly fear and greed), you shouldn't try to time the markets. Knowing when to buy and sell is much harder than you may think.

As a young adult, you're in a position to take more risks because you're investing for the long haul. However, you should be careful that you don't get sucked into investing a lot of your money in aggressive investments that seem to be in a hyped state. Many people don't become aware of an investment until it receives lots of attention. By the time everyone else talks about an investment, it's often nearing or at its peak.

Before you invest in any individual stock, no matter how great a company you think it is, you need to understand the company's line of business, strategies, competitors, financial statements, and P/E ratio versus the competition, among many other issues. Selecting and monitoring good companies take research, time, and discipline.

Also, remember that if a company taps into a product line or way of doing business that proves to be highly successful, that success invites competition. So you need to understand the barriers to entry that a leading company has erected and how difficult or easy it is for competitors to join the fray.

Be wary of analysts' predictions about earnings and stock prices. Analysts, who are too optimistic (as shown in numerous independent studies), have a conflict of interest because the investment banks that they work for seek to cultivate the business (new stock and bond issues) of the companies that they purport to rate and analyze.

Simply buying today's rising and analyst-recommended stocks often leads to future disappointment. If the company's growth slows or the profits don't materialize as expected, the underlying stock price can nosedive.

Psychologically, it's easier for many folks to buy stocks after those stocks have had a huge increase in price. Just as you shouldn't attempt to drive your car looking solely through your rearview mirror, basing investments solely on past performance usually leads novice investors into overpriced investments. If many people talk about the stunning rise in the market, and new investors pile in based on the expectation of hefty profits, tread carefully.

I'm not saying that you need to sell your current stock holdings if you see an investment market getting frothy and speculative. As long as you diversify your stocks worldwide and hold other investments, such as real estate and bonds, the stocks that you hold in one market need to be only a fraction of your total holdings.

Timing the markets is difficult: You can never know how high is high and when it's time to sell, and then how low is low and when it's time to buy. And if you sell non-retirement-account investments at a profit, you end up sacrificing a lot of the profit to federal and state taxes.

Getting past the gloom

During the 2008 financial crisis, panic (and talk of another Great Depression) was in the air, and stock prices dropped sharply.

Peak to trough, global stock prices plunged more than 50 percent. While some companies went under (and garnered lots of news headlines), those firms were few and were the exception rather than the norm. Many terrific companies weathered the storm, and their stock could be scooped up by investors with cash and courage at attractive prices and valuations.

When bad news and pessimism abound and the stock market has dropped, it's actually a much safer and better time to buy stocks. You may even consider shifting some of your money out of your safer investments, such as bonds, and invest more aggressively in stocks. During these times, investors often feel that prices can drop farther, but if you buy and wait, you'll likely be amply rewarded.

Sidestepping common investing minefields

Shares of stock, which represent portions of ownership in companies, offer a way for people of all economic means to invest in companies and build wealth. History shows that long-term investors can win in the stock market because it appreciates over the years. That said, some people who remain active in the market over many years manage to lose some money because of easily avoidable mistakes, which I can keep you from making in the future.

You can greatly increase your chances of investing success and earning higher returns if you avoid the following common stock investing mistakes:

✔ **Broker conflicts:** Some investors make the mistake of investing in individual stocks through a broker who earns commissions. The standard pitch of these firms and their brokers is that they maintain research departments that monitor and report on stocks. Their brokers use this research to tell you when to buy, sell, or hold. It sounds good in theory, but this system has significant problems. Many brokerage firms happen to be in another business that creates enormous conflicts of interest in producing objective company reviews. These investment firms also solicit companies to help them sell new stock and bond issues. To gain this business, the brokerage firms need to demonstrate enthusiasm and optimism for the company's future prospects. Studies of brokerage firms' stock ratings have shown that from a predictive perspective, most of their research is barely worth the cost of the paper that it's printed on.

✓ **Short-term trading:** Unfortunately (for themselves), some investors track their stock investments closely and believe that they need to sell after short holding periods — months, weeks, or even days. With the growth of Internet and computerized trading, such shortsightedness has taken a turn for the worse as more investors now engage in a foolish process known as *day trading,* in which they buy and sell a stock within the same day! Whether you hold a stock for only a few hours or a few months, you're not investing; you're gambling. Specifically, the numerous drawbacks that I see to short-term trading include higher trading costs, more taxes and tax headaches, lower returns from being out of the market when it moves up, and inordinate amounts of time spent researching and monitoring your investments.

✓ **Following gurus:** It's tempting to wish that you could consult a guru who could foresee an impending major decline and get you out of an investment before it tanks. Believe me when I say that plenty of these pundits are talking up such supposed prowess. From having researched many such claims (see the "Guru Watch" section of my website, www.erictyson.com), I can tell you that nearly all these folks significantly misrepresent their past predictions and recommendations. Also, the few who made some halfway-decent predictions in the recent short term had poor or unremarkable longer-term track records. As you develop your investment portfolio, take a level of risk and aggressiveness with which you're comfortable. No pundit has a working crystal ball that can tell you what's going to happen with the economy and financial markets in the future.

Highlighting How to Invest in Stocks

When you invest in stocks, you have lots of options. In addition to the tens of thousands of stocks to choose from, you can invest in mutual funds, exchange-traded funds (ETFs), or hedge funds.

Investing in stock mutual funds and exchange-traded funds

Mutual funds take money invested by people like you and me and pool it in a single investment portfolio in securities, such as stocks and bonds. The portfolio is then professionally managed. Stock mutual funds, as the name suggests, invest primarily or exclusively in stocks. (Some stock funds sometimes invest a bit in other stuff, such as bonds.)

If you're busy and realize your lack of expertise analyzing and picking stocks, you'll love the best stock mutual funds. Investing in stocks through mutual funds can be as simple as dialing a toll-free phone number or logging on to a fund company's website, completing some application forms, and zapping off the money you want to invest.

ETFs are newer versions of mutual funds. The best ETFs are in many ways similar to mutual funds except that they trade on a stock exchange. The chief attractions are those ETFs that offer investors the potential for even lower operating expenses than those of comparable mutual funds.

The best stock mutual funds and ETFs offer numerous advantages:

- ✔ **Diversification:** Buying individual stocks on your own is relatively costly unless you buy reasonable chunks (100 shares or so) of each stock. But to buy 100 shares each of, say, a dozen companies' stocks to ensure diversification, you may need about $60,000 if the stocks that you buy average $50 per share.

- ✔ **Professional management:** Even if you have big bucks to invest, funds offer something that you can't deliver: professional, full-time management. Mutual fund managers peruse a company's financial statements and otherwise track and analyze its business strategy and market position. The best managers put in long hours and possess lots of expertise and experience in the field.

✔ **Low costs:** To convince you that mutual funds and ETFs aren't good ways for you to invest, those with a vested interest, such as stock-picking pundits, may point out the high fees that some funds charge. But high-cost funds aren't the only ones out there. Through a no-load (commission-free) mutual fund or ETF, you can hire a professional, full-time money manager to invest $10,000 for a mere $10 to $50 per year.

Mutual funds and ETFs, of course, have drawbacks:

✔ **Less control:** If you like being in control, sending your investment dollars to a seemingly black-box process in which others decide when and in what to invest your money may unnerve you. However, you should be more concerned about the potential blunders that you may make investing in individual stocks of your own choosing or, even worse, those stocks pitched to you by a broker.

✔ **Taxes:** Taxes are a concern when you invest in mutual funds and ETFs outside retirement accounts. Because the fund manager decides when to sell specific stock holdings, some funds may produce relatively high levels of taxable distributions. But you can use tax-friendly funds and ETFs if taxes concern you.

Picking your own stocks

Plenty of investing blogs, gurus, and books enthusiastically encourage people to do their own stock picking. However, the vast majority of investors are better off not picking their own stocks.

I've long been an advocate of people educating themselves and taking responsibility for their own financial affairs, but taking responsibility for your own finances doesn't mean that you should do everything yourself.

Some popular investing books try to convince investors that they can do a better job than the professionals at picking their own stocks. Amateur investors, however, need to devote a lot of study to become proficient at stock selection. Many professional investors work 80 hours a week at investing, but you're unlikely to be willing or able to spend that much time on it.

Investing through hedge funds

Like mutual funds, hedge funds are managed investment vehicles pitched and available only to higher-net-worth folks. With a hedge fund, there's an investment management team that researches and manages the funds' portfolio. However, hedge funds are oriented toward affluent investors and typically charge steep fees — a 1.0 percent to 1.5 percent annual management fee, plus a 20 percent cut of the annual fund returns. Those high hedge-fund fees depress their returns.

Notwithstanding the small number of hedge funds that have produced better long-term returns, too many affluent folks invest in hedge funds due to the funds' hyped marketing and the badge of exclusivity they offer.

Researching individual stocks

When investing in stocks, I think you're better off sticking to mutual funds and ETFs. In Chapter 10, I dive into far more detail about how to do just that. However, I realize that you may be interested in picking some stocks on your own.

You can spend hundreds of hours researching and reading information on one company alone. Therefore, unless you're financially independent and want to spend nearly all your productive time investing, you need to focus on where you can get the best bang for your buck and time:

- ✔ **The *Value Line Investment Survey:*** Value Line is an investment research company. Value Line's securities analysts have been tracking and researching stocks since 1931. Its analysis and recommendation track record is quite good, and its analysts are beholden to no one. Many professional money managers use the *Value Line Investment Survey,* Value Line's weekly newsletter, as a reference because of its comprehensiveness. Value Line condenses the key information and statistics about a stock and the company behind the stock to a single page.

- ✔ **Independent brokerage research:** If you're going to invest in individual stocks, you need a brokerage account. In addition to offering low trading fees, the best brokerage firms allow you to easily tap into useful research, especially through the firm's website, that you can use to assist with your investing decisions. Because discount brokers aren't in the investment-banking business of working with companies to sell new issues of stock, discount brokers have a level of objectivity in their research reports that traditional brokers (ones like Merrill Lynch, Morgan Stanley, and so on) often lack. Some discount brokers, such as Charles Schwab, produce their own highly regarded research reports, but most discount brokers simply provide reports from independent third parties.

✔ **Successful money managers' stock picks:** To make money in stocks, you certainly don't need an original idea. In fact, it makes sense to examine what the best money managers are buying for their portfolios. Mutual fund managers, for example, are required to disclose at least twice a year what stocks they hold in their portfolios. You can call the best fund companies and ask them to send their most recent semiannual reports that detail their stock holdings, or you can view those reports on many fund companies' websites. Through its website, Morningstar (`www.morning star.com`) allows you to see which mutual funds hold large portions of a given stock that you may be researching and what the success or lack thereof is of the funds that are buying a given stock. Finally, you can follow what Warren Buffett's and other successful investors' funds are buying by visiting the Securities and Exchange Commission website at `www.sec.gov` and looking up specific investment funds' holdings.

✔ **Financial publications and websites:** Many publications and websites cover the world of stocks. But you have to be careful: Just because certain columnists or publications advocate particular stocks or investing strategies doesn't mean that you'll achieve success by following their advice. Publications offering useful columns and commentary, sometimes written by professional money managers, on individual stocks include *Barron's, Business Week, Forbes, Kiplinger's,* and *The Wall Street Journal.* In addition, hundreds of websites are devoted to stock picking. (Visit my site at `www.erictyson.com` for more information.)

✔ **Annual reports:** Publicly traded companies must file certain financial documents annually. Consider reviewing these documents to enhance your understanding of a company's businesses and strategies rather than for the predictive value that you may hope they provide. The annual report is a yearly report that provides standardized financial statements, as well as management's discussion of how the company has performed and how it plans to improve future performance. While some companies have been sued for misleading shareholders with inflated forecasts or lack of disclosure of problems, know that responsible companies try to present a balanced — and, of course, hopeful — perspective in their annual reports.

✔ **10-Ks:** 10-Ks are expanded versions of annual reports. Most investment professionals read the 10-K rather than the annual report because the 10-K contains additional data and information, especially for a company's various divisions and product lines. Also, 10-Ks contain little of the verbal hype that you find in most annual reports. In fact, the 10-K is probably one of the most objective reports that a company publishes. If you're not intimidated by annual reports or if you want more details, read the 10-Ks of the companies you want to check out. 10-Qs provide information similar to 10-Ks, but on a quarterly basis.

✔ **Earnings calls:** Listen to a recent earnings call. Earnings calls allow you to hear from management, as well as listen to the questions that professional analysts ask. Replays are often available on companies' investor-relations websites.

Final thoughts on stock picking

Keep the amount that you dedicate to individual stock investments to a minimum — ideally, no more than 20 percent of your invested dollars. I encourage you to do such investing for the educational value and enjoyment that you derive from it, not because you smugly think you're as skilled as the best professional money managers. Unless you're extraordinarily lucky or unusually gifted at analyzing company and investor behavior, you won't earn above-average returns if you select your own stocks.

Try to buy stock in good-size chunks, such as 100 shares. Otherwise, commissions gobble a large percentage of the small dollar amount that you invest. If you don't have enough money to build a diversified portfolio all at once, don't sweat it. Diversify over time. Purchase shares of one stock after you have enough money accumulated and then wait to buy the next stock until you've saved another chunk of money to invest.

Maximizing Your Stock Market Returns

Anybody, no matter what his or her educational background, IQ, occupation, income, or assets, can make solid returns investing in stocks.

To maximize your chances of stock market investment success, remember the following:

- ✔ **Don't try to time the markets.** Anticipating where the stock market and specific stocks are heading is next to impossible, especially over the short term. Economic factors, which are influenced by thousands of elements as well as human emotions, determine stock market prices. Be a regular buyer of stocks with new savings. As I discuss earlier in this chapter, buy more stocks when prices are down and market pessimism is high.

- ✔ **Diversify your investments.** Invest in the stocks of different-size companies in varying industries around the world. When assessing your investments' performance, examine your whole portfolio at least once a year, and calculate your total return after expenses and trading fees.

- ✔ **Keep trading costs, management fees, and commissions to a minimum.** These costs represent a big drain on your returns. If you invest through an individual broker or a financial advisor who earns a living on commissions, odds are that you're paying more than you need to be, and you're likely receiving biased advice, too.

- ✔ **Pay attention to taxes.** Like commissions and fees, federal and state taxes are major investment expenses that you can minimize. Contribute most of your money to your tax-advantaged retirement accounts. You can invest your money outside retirement accounts, but keep an eye on taxes (see Chapter 4). Calculate your annual returns on an after-tax basis.

- ✔ **Don't overestimate your ability to pick the big-winning stocks.** One of the best ways to invest in stocks is through mutual funds and ETFs, which allow you to use an experienced, full-time money manager at a low cost to perform all the investing grunt work for you (see Chapter 10).

Chapter 9

Securing Investment Income and Principal with Bonds

- -

In This Chapter

▶ Making sense of the various types of bonds

▶ Using bonds in a portfolio

▶ Choosing the best bonds for your situation

- -

*W*hen you invest, it's fun and rewarding to see your investments grow over the years. Riskier investments like stocks and real estate can produce generous long-term returns, well in excess of the rate of inflation. But lending investments like bonds make sense for a portion of your money if

✔ **You expect to sell some of those investments within five years.** Stocks and other growth-oriented investments can fluctuate too much in value to ensure your getting your principal back within five years.

✔ **Investment volatility makes you nervous, or you just want to cushion some of the volatility of your other, riskier investments.** High-quality and shorter-term bonds tend to provide investors a smoother ride.

✔ **You need more current income from your investments.** Bonds tend to produce more income in the short term. That said, you need to be aware that dividend-paying stocks may offer more income over the long term, as their dividends tend to increase over time.

> ✔ **You don't need to make your money grow after infla-
> tion and taxes.** Perhaps you're one of those rare folks
> who has managed to amass a nice-size nest egg at a rela-
> tively young age, and you're less concerned with growing
> that money.

Mind you, all these conditions need not apply for you to put
some of your money into bonds. Also, this list isn't meant
to be an exhaustive list of reasons to invest some money in
bonds.

In this chapter, I discuss how and why to use bonds in your
investment portfolio, explain the different types of bonds as
well as alternatives to bonds, and describe the best ways to
invest in bonds.

Defining Bonds

Bonds are middle-ground investments. They generally offer
higher yields than bank accounts and less volatility than the
stock market. That's why bonds appeal to safety-minded
investors as well as to otherwise-aggressive investors who
seek diversification or investments for short-term financial
goals.

Bonds differ from one another according to several factors:
the entities that issue the bonds (which has important associated tax implications), credit quality, and time to maturity.
After you have a handle on these issues, you're ready to consider investing in bond mutual funds, exchange-traded bond
funds, and perhaps even some individual bonds (although I
caution you especially against jumping into individual bonds,
which can be minefields for inexperienced investors).

Unfortunately, due to shady marketing practices by some
investing companies and bond salespeople, you can have
your work cut out for you while trying to get a handle on what
many bonds really are and how they differ from their peers. I
walk you through how bonds differ from one another in this
section.

Understanding bond issuers

A major dimension in which bonds differ is the organizations that issued the bonds. The issuer of a bond is actually borrowing money from the folks who buy the bonds when they're originally sold.

Who issues a bond is hugely important. First, it determines how likely the bond issuer is to be able to pay back the bonds' principal when the bonds mature. Second, the type of entity doing the bond issuance determines the taxation of the bond's interest payments.

The following list covers the major options for who issues bonds (in order of popularity) and tells you when each option may make sense for you:

- ✔ **Corporate bonds:** Companies such as IBM, McDonald's, and United Technologies issue corporate bonds. Corporate bonds pay interest that's fully taxable at the federal and state levels. Thus, such bonds make sense for investing inside retirement accounts. Lower-tax-bracket investors can consider investing in such bonds outside a tax-sheltered retirement account. (Higher-tax-bracket investors should consider municipal bonds, which appear later in this list.)

- ✔ **Treasury bonds:** Treasuries are issued by the U.S. government. Treasuries pay interest that's state-tax-free but federally taxable. Thus, they make sense if you want to avoid a high state income tax bracket but not a high federal income tax bracket. However, most people in a high state income tax bracket also happen to be in a high federal income tax bracket. Such investors may be better off in municipal bonds (explained next), which are both free of federal and state income tax (in their state of issuance). The best use of Treasuries is in place of bank certificate of deposits (CDs), as both types of investments have government backing. Treasuries that mature in the same length of time as a CD may pay the same interest rate or a better one.

    Bank CD interest is fully taxable, whereas a Treasury's interest is state-tax-free.

✔ **Municipal bonds:** Municipal bonds (muni bonds, for short) are issued by state or local governments. Muni bonds pay interest that's free of federal and state taxes to residents in the state of issue. If you live in New York and buy a bond issued by a New York government agency, you probably won't owe New York state or federal income tax on the interest. The government organizations that issue municipal bonds know that the investors who buy these bonds don't have to pay most or any of the income tax that is normally assessed on other bonds' interest payments. Therefore, the issuing governments can pay a lower rate of interest. If you're in a high tax bracket and want to invest in bonds outside of your tax-sheltered retirement accounts, compare the yield on a given muni bond (or muni bond fund) to the after-tax yield on a comparable taxable bond (or bond fund).

✔ **Convertible bonds:** Convertible bonds are bonds that you can convert under a specified circumstance into a preset number of shares of stock in the company that issued the bond. Although these bonds do pay taxable interest, their yield is lower than that of nonconvertible bonds because convertibles offer you the potential to make more money from the underlying stock.

✔ **International bonds:** You can buy bonds issued by foreign countries. These international bonds are riskier because their interest payments can be offset by currency price changes. The prices of foreign bonds tend not to move in tandem with U.S. bonds. Foreign bond values benefit from, and thus protect against, a declining U.S. dollar; therefore, they offer some diversification value. Although the declining dollar during most of the 2000s boosted the return of foreign bonds, the U.S. dollar appreciated versus most currencies during the 1980s and 1990s, which lowered a U.S. investor's return on foreign bonds.

Foreign bonds aren't vital holdings for a diversified portfolio. They're generally more expensive to purchase and hold than comparable domestic bonds.

Treasury inflation-protected securities (TIPS)

The U.S. government offers bonds called Treasury inflation-protected securities (TIPS). Compared with traditional Treasury bonds, TIPS usually carry a lower interest rate. The reason for this lower rate is that the other portion of your return with these inflation-indexed bonds comes from the inflation adjustment to the principal you invest. The inflation portion of the return gets added back into the principal.

If you invest $10,000 in an inflation-indexed bond, and inflation is 3 percent the first year you hold the bond, your principal increases to $10,300 at the end of the first year.

What's potentially attractive about these bonds is that no matter what happens with the rate of inflation, investors who buy TIPS always earn some return (the yield or interest rate paid) above and beyond the rate of inflation. Thus, holders of inflation-indexed Treasuries can't have the purchasing power of their principal or interest eroded by high inflation.

Because inflation-indexed Treasuries protect investors from the ravages of inflation, they represent less-risky securities. But consider this little-known fact: If the economy experiences deflation (falling prices), your principal isn't adjusted down, so these bonds offer deflation protection as well. (Technically, the principal can't fall below the original par amount, but it can decline back to that level. So if you buy a TIP that was issued a while ago and it has had the principal factored higher due to inflation, you could suffer a declining principal if deflation occurs.)

Considering credit (default) risk

Closely tied to what organizations are actually issuing the bonds, bonds also differ in the creditworthiness of their issuers. Credit rating agencies such as Moody's, Standard & Poor's, and Fitch rate the credit quality and likelihood of default of bonds.

The credit rating of a bond depends on the issuer's ability to pay back its debt. Bond credit ratings are usually done on some sort of a letter-grade scale. AAA usually is the highest rating, and ratings descend through AA and A, followed by BBB, BB, B, CCC, CC, C, and so on.

✔ **AAA- and AA-rated bonds** are considered to be high-grade or high-credit-quality bonds. Such bonds possess little chance of default (a fraction of 1 percent).

✔ **A- and BBB-rated bonds** are considered to be investment-grade or general-quality bonds.

✔ **BB- or lower-rated bonds** are known as junk bonds (or as their marketed name, high-yield bonds). Junk bonds, also known as non-investment-grade bonds, are more likely to default; perhaps as many as 2 percent per year actually default.

To minimize investing in bonds that default, purchase highly rated bonds. Now, you might ask why investors would knowingly buy a bond with a low credit rating. They may purchase one of these bonds because the issuer pays a higher interest rate on lower-quality bonds to attract investors. The lower a bond's credit rating and quality, the higher the yield you can and should expect from such a bond.

Poorer-quality bonds aren't for the faint of heart, because they're generally volatile in value. I don't recommend buying individual junk bonds; consider investing in these only through a well-run junk-bond fund. (Keep in mind that the volatility profile for a junk-bond fund is closer to stocks than it is for high-grade corporate bonds.)

Making sense of bond maturities

Bonds are generally classified by the length of time until maturity. *Maturity* simply means the time at which the bond promises to pay back your principal if you hold the bond. Maturity could be next year, in 7 years, in 15 years, and so on.

Bonds classifications are as follows:

✔ **Short-term bonds** mature in the next few years.

✔ **Intermediate-term bonds** come due within three to ten years.

✔ **Long-term bonds** mature in more than 10 years and generally up to 30 years.

A small number of companies (such as Coca-Cola, Disney, and IBM) issue 100-year bonds. I don't recommend buying such bonds, however, especially those issued during a period of low interest rates, because they get hammered if long-term interest rates spike higher.

You should care how long a bond takes to mature because maturity gives you some sense of how volatile a bond may be if overall market interest rates change. If interest rates fall, bond prices rise; if interest rates rise, bond prices fall. Longer-term bonds generally drop more in price when the overall level of interest rates rises.

If you hold a bond until it matures, you get your principal back unless the issuer defaults. In the meantime, however, if interest rates rise, bond prices fall. The reason is simple: If the bond that you hold is issued at, say, 4 percent, and interest rates on similar bonds rise to 5 percent, no one (except someone who doesn't know any better) will want to purchase your 4 percent bond. The value of your bond has to decrease enough so that it effectively yields 5 percent.

Most of the time, long-term bonds pay higher yields than short-term bonds do. You can look at a chart of the current yield of similar bonds plotted against when they mature — a chart known as a *yield curve*. At most times, this curve slopes upward. Investors generally demand a higher rate of interest for taking the risk of holding longer-term bonds.

Using Bonds in a Portfolio

Investing in bonds is a time-honored way to earn a better rate of return on money that you don't plan to use within the next couple of years or more. Like stocks, bonds can generally be sold any day that the financial markets are open.

In this section I discuss how to use bonds as an investment and explain how bonds compare with other lending investments.

Finding uses for bonds

Because their value fluctuates, you're more likely to lose money if you're forced to sell your bonds sooner rather than later. In the short term, if the bond market happens to fall and you need to sell, you could lose money. In the long term, as is the case with stocks, you're far less likely to lose money.

Following are some common situations in which investing in bonds can make sense:

- ✔ **You're looking to make a major purchase.** This purchase should be one that won't happen for at least two years. Examples include buying a car or a home. Short-term bonds may work for you as a higher-yielding and slightly riskier alternative to money market funds.

- ✔ **You want to diversify your portfolio.** Bonds don't move in perfect tandem with the performance of other types of investments, such as stocks. In fact, in a poor economic environment (such as during the Great Depression of the 1930s or the financial crisis of the late 2000s), bonds may appreciate in value while riskier investments such as stocks decline.

- ✔ **You're interested in diversifying your long-term investments.** You may invest some of your money in bonds as part of a long-term investment strategy, such as for retirement. You should have an overall plan for how you want to invest your money (see Chapter 2). Aggressive younger investors should keep less of their retirement money in bonds than older folks who are nearing retirement.

- ✔ **You need income-producing investments.** When you're retired (probably much later in life) or not working, bonds can be useful because they're better at producing current income than many other investments.

I don't recommend putting your emergency cash reserve in bonds. That's what a money market fund or bank savings/credit union account is for (see Chapters 6 and 7).

Don't put too much of your long-term investment money in bonds, either. Bonds are generally inferior investments for making your money grow. Growth-oriented investments — such as stocks, real estate, and your own business — hold the greatest potential to build real wealth.

Comparing other lending investments with bonds

As I explain in Chapter 1, lending investments are those in which you lend your money to an organization, such as a bank, company, or government, that typically pays you a set or fixed rate of interest. Ownership investments, by contrast, provide partial ownership of a company or some other asset, such as real estate, that has the ability to generate revenue and potential profits.

Lending investments aren't the best choice if you really want to make your money grow, but even the most aggressive investors should consider placing some of their money in lending investments.

In this chapter, I focus on bonds, but I'd be remiss if I failed to point out that lending investments are everywhere: banks, credit unions, brokerage firms, insurance companies, and mutual fund companies. Lending investments that you may have heard of include bank accounts (savings and CDs), Treasury bills and other bonds, bond mutual funds and exchange-traded bond funds, mortgages, and *guaranteed- investment contracts* (GICs).

Bonds, money market funds, and bank savings vehicles are hardly the only lending investments. A variety of other companies are more than willing to have you lend them your money and pay you a relatively fixed rate of interest. In most cases, though, you're better off staying away from the investments described in the following sections.

Too many investors get sucked into lending investments that offer higher yields and are pitched as supposedly better alternatives to bonds. Remember: Risk and return go hand in hand, so higher yields mean greater risk, and vice versa.

One of the allures of nonbond lending investments, such as private mortgages, GICs, and CDs, is that they don't fluctuate in value — at least not that you can see. Such investments appear to be safer and less volatile. You can't watch your principal fluctuate in value because you can't look up the value daily, the way you can with bonds and stocks.

But the principal values of your mortgage, GIC, and CD investments really do fluctuate; you just don't see the fluctuations! Just as the market value of a bond drops when interest rates rise, so does the market value of these investments — and for the same reasons. At higher interest rates, investors expect a discounted price on a fixed-interest-rate investment because they always have the alternative of purchasing a new mortgage, GIC, or CD at the higher prevailing rates. Some of these investments are actually bought and sold, and behave just like bonds, among investors in what's known as a secondary market.

If the normal volatility of a bond's principal value makes you uneasy, try not to follow your investments so closely!

In the sections that follow, I explain common lending investments that are often pitched as bond alternatives with supposedly more stable prices. You can find information on CDs in Chapter 6.

Guaranteed-investment contracts (GICs)

Through your retirement plan at work, you may be pitched to invest in *guaranteed-investment contracts* (GICs). The allure of GICs, which are sold and backed by insurance companies, is that your account value doesn't appear to fluctuate. (Other insurer-backed investments sold to the public through brokers are similar.) Like one-year bank CDs, GICs generally quote you an interest rate for the next year. Some GICs lock in the rate for longer periods, whereas others may change the interest rate several times per year.

Keep in mind that the insurance company that issues the GIC does invest your money, mostly in bonds and maybe a bit in stocks. Like other bonds and stocks, these investments fluctuate in value; you just don't see the fluctuation.

Typically once a year, you receive a new statement showing that your GIC is worth more, thanks to the newly added interest. This statement makes otherwise-nervous investors who can't stand volatile investments feel safe and sound.

The yield on a GIC is usually comparable to those available on short-term, high-quality bonds, yet the insurer invests in long-term bonds and some stocks. The difference between what these investments generate for the insurer and what the GIC pays you in interest goes to the insurer.

The insurer's take can be significant and is generally hidden. Mutual funds are required to report the management fees that they collect and subtract before paying your return, but GIC insurers have no such obligations. By having a return guaranteed in advance (with no chance for loss), you pay heavily — an effective fee of more than 2 percent per year — for peace of mind in the form of lower long-term returns.

The high effective fees that you pay to have an insurer manage your money in a GIC aren't the only drawbacks. When you invest in a GIC, your assets are part of the insurer's general assets. Insurance companies sometimes fail, and although they often merge with healthy insurers, you can still lose money. The rate of return on GICs from a failed insurance company is often slashed to help restore financial soundness to the company. So the only "guarantee" that comes with a GIC is that the insurer agrees to pay you the promised rate of interest as long as it is able.

Private mortgages

To invest in mortgages directly, you can loan your money to people who need money to buy or refinance real estate. Such loans are known as *private mortgages,* or *second mortgages* if your loan is second in line behind someone's primary mortgage.

You may be pitched to invest in a private mortgage by folks you know in real estate-related businesses. Mortgage and real estate brokers often arrange mortgage investments, and you must tread carefully, because these people have a vested interest in seeing the deal done. Otherwise, the mortgage broker doesn't get paid for closing the loan, and the real estate broker doesn't get a commission for selling a property.

Private mortgage investments appeal to investors who don't like the volatility of the stock and bond markets and who aren't satisfied with the seemingly low returns on bonds or other common lending investments. Private mortgages appear to offer the best of both worlds — stock-market-like returns without the volatility that comes with stocks.

One broker who also happens to write about real estate wrote a newspaper column describing mortgages as the "perfect real estate investment" and added that mortgages are a "high-yield, low-risk investment." If that wasn't enough to get you to whip out your checkbook, the writer/broker further gushed that mortgages are great investments because you have "little or no management, no physical labor."

You may know by now that a low-risk, high-yield investment doesn't exist. Earning a relatively high interest rate goes hand in hand with accepting relatively high risk. The risk is that the borrower can default — which leaves you holding the bag. (In the mid- to late 2000s, mortgage defaults skyrocketed.) More specifically, you can get stuck with a property that you may need to foreclose on, and if you don't hold the first mortgage, you're not first in line with a claim on the property.

The fact that private mortgages are high-risk should be obvious when you consider why the borrower elects to obtain needed funds privately rather than through a bank. Put yourself in the borrower's shoes. As a property buyer or owner, if you can obtain a mortgage through a conventional lender, such as a bank, wouldn't you do so? After all, banks generally give better interest rates. If a mortgage broker offers you a deal where you can, for example, borrow money at 10 percent when the going bank rate is, say, 6 percent, the deal must carry a fair amount of risk.

I recommend that you generally avoid investing in private mortgages. If you really want to invest in such mortgages, you must do some time-consuming homework on the borrower's financial situation. A banker doesn't lend someone money without examining a borrower's assets, liabilities, and monthly expenses, and you shouldn't either. Be careful to check the borrower's credit, and get a large down payment (at least 20 percent). The best circumstance in which to be a lender is if you sell some of your own real estate, and you're willing to act as the bank and provide the financing to the buyer in the form of a first mortgage.

Also recognize that your mortgage investment carries interest-rate risk: If you need to "sell" it early, you'll have to discount it, perhaps substantially if interest rates have increased since you purchased it. Try not to lend so much money on one mortgage that it represents more than 5 percent of your total investments.

If you're willing to lend your money to borrowers who carry a relatively high risk of defaulting, consider investing in high-yield (junk) bond mutual funds or exchange-traded funds instead (see Chapter 10). With these funds, you can at least diversify your money across many borrowers, and you benefit from the professional review and due diligence of the fund management team. You can also consider lending money to family members.

How and Where to Invest in Bonds

You can invest in bonds in one of two major ways: You can invest in a professionally selected and managed portfolio of bonds via a bond mutual fund or exchange-traded fund (ETF), or you can purchase individual bonds.

In this section, I help you make the decision of how to invest in bonds. If you want to take the individual-bond route, I cover that path here, including the purchasing process for various types of bonds such as Treasuries, which are different in that you can buy them directly from the government. If you fall on the side of mutual funds and ETFs, see Chapter 10 for all the details.

Choosing between bond funds and individual bonds

Unless the bonds you're considering purchasing are easy to analyze and homogeneous (such as Treasury bonds), you're generally better off investing in bonds through a mutual fund or ETF. Here's why:

- **Diversification is easy with funds and much more difficult with individual bonds.** You shouldn't put your money in a small number of bonds of companies in the same industry or that mature at the same time. It's difficult to cost-effectively build a diversified bond portfolio with individual issues unless you have more than $1 million that you want to invest in bonds.

✔ **The best funds are cost-effective; individual bonds cost you more money.** Great bond funds are yours for less than 0.5 percent per year in operating expenses (see Chapter 10). If you purchase individual bonds through a broker, you're going to pay a commission. In most cases, the commission cost is hidden; the broker quotes you a price for the bond that includes the commission. Even if you use a discount broker, these fees take a healthy bite out of your investment. The smaller the amount that you invest, the bigger the percentage bite. On a $1,000 bond, the commission fee can equal several percent.

✔ **You have better things to do with your time than research bonds and go bond shopping.** Bonds are boring, and bonds and the companies that stand behind them aren't simple to understand. Did you know, for example, that some bonds can be called before their maturity dates? Companies often call bonds, which means they repay the principal before maturity, to save money if interest rates drop significantly. After you purchase a bond, you need to do the same things that a good bond fund portfolio manager needs to do, such as track the issuer's creditworthiness and monitor other important financial developments. In addition to the direction of overall interest rates, changes in the financial health of the issuing entity company that stands behind the bond strongly affect the price of an individual bond.

Investing in Treasury bonds

If you want to purchase Treasury bonds, buying them through the Federal Reserve's Treasury Direct program online is generally the lowest-cost method. The Federal Reserve doesn't charge for buying Treasuries through these online accounts. Contact a Federal Reserve branch near you (check the government section of your local phone directory), and ask for information about how to purchase Treasury bonds through the Treasury Direct program. Or you can call 800-722-2678 or visit the U.S. Department of the Treasury's website (www.treasurydirect.gov).

You may also purchase and hold Treasury bonds through brokerage firms and mutual funds. Brokers typically charge a flat fee for buying a Treasury bond. Buying Treasuries through a brokerage account makes sense if you hold other securities through the brokerage account and you like the ability to quickly sell a Treasury bond that you hold. Selling Treasury bonds held through the Federal Reserve is a hassle, as you must transfer the bonds out to a broker to do the selling for you.

The advantage of a fund that invests in Treasuries is that it typically holds Treasuries of differing maturities, thus offering diversification. You can generally buy and sell no-load (commission-free) Treasury bond funds easily and without fees. Funds, however, do charge an ongoing management fee. (See Chapter 10 for my recommendations of Treasury mutual funds with good track records and low management fees.)

Investing in non-Treasury individual bonds

Purchasing other types of individual bonds, such as corporate and mortgage bonds, is a much more treacherous and time-consuming undertaking than buying Treasuries. Here's my advice for doing it right and minimizing the chance of mistakes:

- **Buy quality, not yield.** Yes, junk bonds pay higher yields, but they also have a much higher chance of default. Also, did you know what a subprime mortgage was before it was all over the news that defaults were on the rise? (*Subprime* mortgages are mortgage loans made to borrowers with lower credit ratings who pay higher interest rates because of their higher risk of default.) You're not a professional money manager who's trained to spot problems and red flags; stick with highly rated bonds so that you don't have to worry about and suffer through these unfortunate consequences.

- **Diversify.** Invest in and hold bonds from a variety of companies in different industries to buffer changes in the economy that adversely affect one industry or a few industries more than others. Of the money that you want to invest in bonds, don't put more than 5 percent in any one bond. Diversification requires a large amount to invest, given the size of most bonds, and trading fees erode your investment balance if you invest too little. If you can't achieve this level of diversification, use a bond mutual fund.

✔ **Understand that bonds may be called early.** Many bonds, especially corporate bonds, can legally be called before maturity. In this case, the bond issuer pays you back early because it doesn't need to borrow as much money or because interest rates have fallen and the borrower wants to issue new bonds at a lower interest rate. Be especially careful about purchasing bonds that were issued at higher interest rates than those that currently prevail. Borrowers pay off such bonds first.

✔ **Shop around.** Just like when you buy a car, shop around for good prices on the bonds that you have in mind. The hard part is doing an apples-to-apples comparison, because brokers may not offer exactly the same bonds. Remember that the two biggest determinants of what a bond should yield are its maturity date and its credit rating. Beware of using commission-based brokers. Many of the worst bond-investing disasters have befallen customers of such brokerage firms. Your best bet is to purchase individual bonds through discount brokers.

Evaluating individual bonds that you currently hold

Perhaps you've already bought some bonds or inherited them. If you already own individual bonds, and they fit your financial objectives and tax situation, you can hold them until maturity, because you already paid a commission when you purchased them. Selling the bonds before their maturity would just create an additional fee. (When the bonds mature, the broker who sold them to you will probably be more than happy to sell you some more. That's the time to check out good bond funds — see Chapter 10.)

Don't mistakenly think that your current individual bonds pay the yield that they had when they were originally issued. That yield is the number listed in the name of the bond on your brokerage account statement. As the market level of interest rates changes, the *effective yield* (the interest payment divided by the bond's price) on your bonds fluctuates to rise and fall with the market level of rates for similar bonds. So if rates have fallen since you bought your bonds, the value of those bonds has increased — which in turn reduces the effective yield that you're earning on your invested dollars.

Chapter 10

Investing in Funds: Mutual Funds and Exchange-Traded Funds

In This Chapter

▶ Matching funds to meet your objectives

▶ Creating and managing a fund portfolio

▶ Exploring alternatives to funds

*T*his chapter is all about investing through funds — mutual funds and exchange-traded funds (ETFs). Mutual funds are simply pools of money from investors that a mutual fund manager uses to buy a bunch of stocks, bonds, and other assets that meet the fund's investment criteria. The best ETFs are quite similar to mutual funds — specifically, index mutual funds. Each ETF generally tracks a major market index. (Some ETFs, however, track narrowly focused indexes, such as an industry group or small country.) The most significant difference between a mutual fund and an ETF is that to invest in an EFT, you must buy it through a stock exchange where the ETFs trade, just as individual stocks trade.

Different types of funds can help you meet various financial goals. You can use money market funds for something most everybody needs: an emergency savings stash of three to six months' living expenses. Or perhaps you're thinking about saving for a home purchase, retirement, or future educational costs. If so, you can consider some stock and bond funds.

Because efficient funds take most of the hassle and cost out of deciding which companies to invest in, they're among the finest investment vehicles available today. Also, funds enable you to have some of the best money managers in the country direct the investment of your money.

In this chapter, I discuss how to match funds to your investing objectives and assemble a portfolio of funds. I also cover alternatives to funds.

Understanding the Advantages of Funds

The best funds are superior investment vehicles for people of all economic means, and they can help you accomplish many financial objectives. The following list highlights the main reasons for investing in funds rather than in individual securities. (If you want to invest in individual stocks, see Chapter 8.)

- **Low cost:** When you invest your money in an efficiently managed fund, it should cost you less than trading individual securities on your own. Fund managers can buy and sell securities for a fraction of the cost that you pay. Funds also spread the cost of research over many, many investors. The most efficiently managed mutual funds cost less than 1 percent per year in fees. (Bonds and money market funds cost much less — in the neighborhood of 0.5 percent per year or less.) Some of the larger and more established funds can charge annual fees less than 0.2 percent per year; that's less than a $2 annual charge per $1,000 you invest.

- **Diversification:** Funds generally invest in dozens of securities. Diversification is a big attraction for many investors who choose funds because proper diversification increases the chance that the fund will earn higher returns with less risk. Most funds own stocks or bonds from dozens of companies, thus diversifying against the risk of bad news from any single company or sector. Achieving such diversification on your own is difficult and expensive unless you have a few hundred thousand dollars and a great deal of time to invest.

✔ **Professional management:** Fund investment companies hire a portfolio manager and researchers whose full-time jobs are to analyze and purchase suitable investments for the fund. These people screen the universe of investments for those that meet the fund's stated objectives. Fund managers are typically graduates of the top business and finance schools, where they learned portfolio management, securities valuation, and securities selection. Many have additional investing credentials, such as Chartered Financial Analyst (CFA) certification. The best fund managers also typically possess more than ten years' experience analyzing and selecting investments.

For fund managers and researchers, finding the best investments is a full-time job. They do major analysis that you lack the time or expertise to perform. Their activities include assessing company financial statements; interviewing company managers to hear the companies' business strategies and vision; examining competitors' strategies; speaking with companies' customers, suppliers, and industry consultants; attending trade shows; and reading industry periodicals.

✔ **Achievable investment minimums:** Many mutual funds have minimums of $1,000 or less. Retirement-account investors can often invest with even less. Some funds even offer monthly investment plans so you can start with as little as $50 per month. ETFs are even better in this department because there are no minimums, although you need to weigh the brokerage costs of buying and selling ETF shares.

✔ **Funds to fit varying needs:** You can select funds that match the ratio of risk to reward you need to meet your financial goals. If you want your money to grow over a long period, and if you can handle down as well as up years, choose stock-focused funds. If you need current income and don't want investments that fluctuate as widely in value as stocks do, consider some bond funds. If you want to be sure that your invested principal doesn't decline in value because you may need to use your money in the short term, select a money market fund. Most investors choose a combination of these types of funds to diversify and to accomplish different financial goals.

✔ **High financial safety:** Fund companies can't fail because the value of fund shares fluctuates as the securities in the fund rise and fall in value. For every dollar of securities that they hold for their customers, mutual funds have a dollar's worth of securities. The worst that can happen with a fund is that if you want your money, you may get less money than you originally put into the fund due to a market value decline of the fund's holdings — but you won't lose all your original investment. For added security, the specific stocks, bonds, and other securities that a mutual fund buys are held by a *custodian,* a separate organization independent of the mutual fund company. A custodian ensures that the fund management company can't abscond with your funds.

✔ **Accessibility:** Funds are set up for people who value their time and don't like going to a local branch office and standing in long lines. You can fill out a simple form (often online, if you want) and write a check in the comfort of your home (or authorize electronic transfers from your bank or other accounts) to make your initial investment. Then you typically can make subsequent investments by mailing in a check or sending money electronically. Many fund companies also allow you to transfer money electronically back and forth from your bank account. Selling shares of your mutual fund usually is simple, too. Generally, all you need to do is call the fund company's toll-free number or visit its website to make the arrangements.

Maximizing Your Chances for Fund Investing Success

I recommend using some straightforward, common-sense, easy-to-use criteria when selecting funds to greatly increase your chances of fund investing success. The criteria presented in this section have proved to dramatically increase your fund investing returns. (My website, www.erictyson.com, has details on research and studies that validate these criteria.)

Understanding the importance of performance and risk

A common and often costly mistake that many investors make when they select a fund is overemphasizing the importance of past performance. The shorter the time period you analyze, the greater the danger that you'll misuse high past performance as an indicator for a fund's likely future performance.

High past returns for a fund, relative to its peers, are largely possible only if a fund takes more risk or if a fund manager's particular investment style happens by luck to come into favor for a few years. The danger of a fund's taking greater risk in the pursuit of market-beating and peer-beating returns is that it doesn't always work the way you hope. The odds are high that you won't be able to pick the next star before it vaults to prominence in the fund universe. You're more likely to jump into a recently high-performing fund and then be along for the ride when it plummets back to reality.

Funds make themselves look better by comparing themselves with funds that aren't really comparable. The most common ploy starts with a manager investing in riskier types of securities; then the fund company, in its marketing, compares its performance with that of fund companies that invest in less-risky securities. Always examine the types of securities that a fund invests in and then make sure that the comparison funds or indexes invest in similar securities.

A fund's historic rate of return or performance is one of several important factors to examine when you select funds. Keep in mind that — as all fund materials must tell you — past performance is no guarantee of future results. In fact, many former high-return funds achieved their results only by taking on high risk or simply by relying on short-term luck. Funds that assume higher risk should produce higher rates of return, but high-risk funds usually decline in price faster during market declines.

Examining fund management experience

Although the individual fund manager is important, a manager isn't an island unto himself. The resources and capabilities of the parent company are equally, if not more, important. Managers come and go, but fund companies usually don't.

Different companies maintain different capabilities and levels of expertise with different types of funds. A fund company gains more or less experience than others not only from the direct management of certain fund types, but also through hiring out. Some fund families contract with private money management firms that possess significant experience. In other cases, private money management firms with long histories in private money management — such as Dodge & Cox, PIMCO, and Tweedy, Browne — offer funds to the general public.

Keeping costs down

The charges that you pay to buy or sell a fund, as well as the ongoing fund operating expenses, have a major effect on the return that you ultimately earn on your fund investments. Given the enormous number of choices available for a particular type of fund, there's no reason to pay high costs.

Fund costs are an important factor in the return that you earn from a fund because fees are deducted from your investment returns. High fees and other charges depress your returns. Here's what I recommend that you do regarding fees:

✔ **Minimize operating expenses.** All funds charge fees as long as you keep your money in the fund. The fees pay for the costs of running a fund, such as employees' salaries, marketing, toll-free phone lines, and writing and publishing prospectuses (the legal disclosure of the fund's operations and fees). A fund's operating expenses are invisible to you because they're deducted from the fund's share price on a daily basis. Funds with higher operating expenses tend to produce lower rates of return on average. Conversely, funds with lower operating costs can more easily produce higher returns for you than comparable types of funds with high costs. This effect makes sense because companies deduct operating expenses from the returns that your fund generates.

Fund companies quote a fund's operating expenses as a percentage of your investment. The percentage represents an annual fee or charge. You can find this number in the fund expense section of a fund's prospectus, usually on a line that says "Total Fund Operating Expense." You also can call the fund's toll-free phone number and ask a representative, or you can find the information at the fund company's website. Make sure that a fund doesn't have lower expenses simply because it's waiving them temporarily. (You can ask the fund representative or look at the fees in the fund's prospectus to find this information.)

✔ **Use no-load funds.** A *sales load* is a commission paid to brokers and financial planners who work on commission and sell loaded mutual funds. Commissions, or *loads,* generally are about 5 percent of the amount that you invest. Sales loads are additional and unnecessary costs that are deducted from your investment money. You can find plenty of outstanding *no-load* (commission-free) funds. I recommend a few later in this chapter.

Invest in funds that have low total operating expenses and that don't charge sales loads. Both types of fees come out of your pocket and reduce your rate of return. Plenty of excellent funds are available at reasonable annual operating-expense ratios (less than 1 percent for stock funds and less than 0.5 percent for bond funds). See my recommendations of specific funds later in this chapter.

Note: Many of the Vanguard funds recommended in this chapter offer Admiral versions that have even lower operating fees for customers who invest at least $100,000 ($50,000, if the account has been in existence for at least ten years, or $10,000 for an index fund that offers Admiral shares).

Understanding and using index funds

In some funds, the portfolio manager and a team of analysts scour the market for the best securities. An index fund manager, however, simply invests to match the makeup — and, thus, the performance — of an index such as the Standard & Poor's 500 index of 500 large U.S.-company stocks. Index funds operate with far lower operating expenses because research isn't needed to identify companies in which to invest.

Index funds deliver relatively solid returns by keeping expenses low, staying invested, and not changing investments. With actively managed stock funds, a fund manager can make costly mistakes, such as not being invested when the market goes up, being too aggressive when the market plummets, or just being in the wrong stocks. An actively managed fund can easily underperform the overall market index that it's competing against. Over ten years or more, index funds typically outperform about three quarters of their peers. Most so-called actively managed funds can't overcome the handicap of high operating expenses that pull down their rates of return.

In addition to lower operating expenses, which help boost your returns, index funds are usually tax-friendlier to invest in when you invest outside retirement accounts. Fund managers of actively managed portfolios, in their attempts to increase returns, buy and sell securities more frequently. This trading, however, increases a fund's taxable capital gains distributions and reduces a fund's after-tax return.

Vanguard is the largest and most successful provider of index funds because it maintains the lowest annual operating fees in the business. Vanguard has all types of bond and stock (both U.S. and international) index funds. See my recommended-fund sections later in this chapter.

Understanding exchange-traded funds: Index funds that trade

Index mutual funds, which track particular market indexes and the best of which feature low costs, have been around for decades. Exchange-traded funds (ETFs) represent a twist on index funds. ETFs trade as stocks do and offer some potential advantages over traditional mutual funds, but they also have some potential drawbacks.

As with index funds, the promise of ETFs is low management fees. I say *promise* because the vast majority of ETFs actually have expense ratios far higher than those of the best index funds.

In addition to slightly lower expenses, the best ETFs have one possible advantage over traditional index funds: Because ETFs may not be forced to redeem shares to cash and recognize taxable gains (which can happen with an index fund), they may be tax-friendlier for non-retirement-account investors.

If you can't meet the minimum investment amounts for index funds (typically, several thousand dollars), you face no minimums when buying an ETF, but you must factor in the brokerage costs of buying and selling ETF shares through your favorite brokerage firm. Suppose that you pay a $10 transaction fee through an online broker to buy $1,000 worth of an ETF. That $10 may not sound like much, but it represents 1 percent of your investment and wipes out the supposed cost advantage of investing in an ETF. Because of the brokerage costs, ETFs aren't good vehicles for investors who seek to make regular monthly investments.

Here are some drawbacks of ETFs:

- ✓ **The perils of market timing:** Being able to trade in and out of an ETF during the trading day presents challenges. In my experience working with individual investors, most people find it both nerve-racking and futile to try to time their moves in and out of stocks with the inevitable fluctuations that take place during the trading day. In theory, traders want to believe that they can buy at relatively low prices and sell at relatively high prices, but that's far easier said than done.

- ✓ **Brokerage commission every time you trade:** With no-load index funds, you generally don't pay fees to buy and sell. With ETFs, however, because you're actually placing a trade on a stock exchange, you generally pay a brokerage commission every time you trade. (*Note:* Some brokers offer certain ETFs without brokerage charges in the hope of getting your account and making money on other investments.)

- ✓ **Fluctuating prices:** Because ETFs fluctuate in price based on supply and demand, when you place a trade during the trading day, you face the complication of trying to determine whether the current price on an ETF is above or below the actual value. With an index fund, you know that the price at which your trade was executed equals the exact market value of the securities it holds.

✔ **Poorly diversified investments:** Many ETFs invest in narrow segments, such as one specific industry or one foreign country. Such funds undermine the diversification value of fund investing and tend to have relatively high fees.

✔ **Excessive risks and costs with leverage:** ETF issuers have come out with increasingly risky and costly ETFs. One particular class of ETFs that I especially dislike consists of so-called leveraged ETFs. These ETFs claim to magnify the move of a particular index, such as the Standard & Poor's 500 stock index, by double or triple. So a double-leveraged S&P 500 ETF is supposed to increase by 2 percent for every 1 percent increase in the S&P 500 index. My investigations of whether the leveraged ETFs actually deliver on their objectives show that they don't — in fact, they don't even come close. Leveraged ETFs aren't investments; they're gambling instruments for day traders.

Creating and Managing a Fund Portfolio

When you invest money for the longer term, such as for retirement, you can choose among the various types of funds that I discuss in this chapter. Most people get a big headache when they try to decide how to spread their money among the choices. This section helps you begin cutting through the clutter for longer-term investing. (I discuss recommended funds for shorter-term goals later in this chapter as well.)

Asset allocation simply means that you decide what percentage of your investments you place, or *allocate,* in bonds versus stocks and international stocks versus U.S. stocks. Asset allocation can include other assets, such as real estate and small business, which are discussed throughout this book.

In your 20s and 30s, time is on your side, and you should use that time to your advantage. You may have many decades before you need to draw on some portion of your retirement-account assets, for example. If some of your investments drop over a year or even over several years, the value of your investments has plenty of time to recover before you spend the money during retirement.

Your current age and the number of years until you retire are the biggest factors in your allocation decision. The younger you are and the more years you have before retirement, the more comfortable you should be with volatile, growth-oriented investments, such as stock funds.

Table 10-1 provides my guidelines for allocating fund money that you've earmarked for long-term purposes, such as retirement. It's a simple but powerful formula that uses your age and the level of risk you're willing to take with your investments.

Table 10-1 Longer-Term Fund Asset Allocation

Your Investment Attitude	Bond Fund Allocation (%)	Stock Fund Allocation (%)
Play it safe	= Age	= 100 – Age
Middle of the road	= Age – 10	= 110 – Age
Aggressive	= Age – 20	= 120 – Age

Suppose that you're an aggressive type who prefers taking a fair amount of risk to make your money grow faster. Using Table 10-1, if you're 30 years old, consider putting 10 percent (30 – 20) into bond funds and 90 percent (120 – 30) into stock funds.

Now divvy up your stock investment money between U.S. and international funds. Here are the portions of your stock allocation that I recommend investing in overseas stocks:

 ✔ 20 percent for a play-it-safe attitude

 ✔ 35 percent for a middle-of-the-road attitude

 ✔ 50 percent for an aggressive attitude

If, in Table 10-1, the 30-year-old aggressive type invests 90 percent in stocks, then she can invest about 50 percent of the stock fund investments (which works out to be around 45 percent of the total) in international stock funds.

So here's what the 30-year-old aggressive investor's portfolio asset allocation looks like:

Bonds	10 percent
U.S. stocks	45 percent
International stocks	45 percent

Suppose that your investment allocation decisions suggest that you invest 50 percent in U.S. stock funds. Which ones do you choose? As I explain in "Picking the best stock funds," later in this chapter, stock funds differ on several levels. You can choose among growth-oriented stocks and funds and those that focus on value stocks, as well as funds that focus on small-, medium-, or large-company stocks. I explain these types of stocks and funds later in this chapter. You also need to decide what portion you want to invest in index funds versus actively managed funds that try to beat the market.

Deciding how much you should use index versus actively managed funds is really a matter of personal taste. If you're satisfied knowing that you'll get the market rate of return and that you can't underperform the market (after accounting for your costs), index your entire portfolio. On the other hand, if you enjoy the challenge of trying to pick the better managers and want the potential to earn better than the market level of returns, don't use index funds at all. Investing in a happy medium of both, as I do, is always a safe bet.

Identifying the Best Mutual Funds and ETFs

In this section, I explain the different types of funds — stock, bond, and money market — and where to find the best ones. Remember that with stock funds and bond funds, you have the option of investing in ETFs as well as traditional mutual funds.

Investing in the best ETFs

Like the vast majority of investors, you don't need to complicate your life by investing in ETFs. Use them only if you're an advanced investor who understands index funds and you've found a superior ETF for a given index fund that you're interested in.

I strongly encourage you to employ the buy-and-hold mentality that I advocate throughout this book. Don't hop in and out of ETFs. Also, you should buy only the ETFs that track the broader market indexes and that have the lowest expense ratios. Avoid those that track narrow industry groups or single small countries.

Check whether the ETF you're considering is selling at a premium or discount to its net asset value. You can find this information on the ETF provider's website after the market's close each business day.

The best ETFs, like the best index funds, have low expense ratios. My top picks among the leading providers of ETFs include the following:

- ✔ **Vanguard:** Historically, Vanguard has been the low-cost leader with index funds, and now it has low-cost ETFs as well. If you're interested in finding out more about ETFs, be sure to examine Vanguard's ETFs. Vanguard also offers the Admiral Share class for bigger-balance customers (more than $100,000) of its index funds that match the low expense ratio on its ETFs. (`https://personal.vanguard.com/us/home`; 800-662-7447)

- ✔ **WisdomTree:** Developed by Wharton business professor Jeremy Siegel, this family of indexes is weighted toward stocks paying higher dividends. These ETFs have higher fees but offer a broad family of index choices for investors seeking stocks that pay higher dividends. ***Note:*** Other ETF providers offer several value-oriented and high-dividend-paying stock funds. (`www.wisdomtree.com`; 866-909-9473)

Picking the best stock funds

Stock funds differ from one another in several dimensions. The following characteristics are what you need to pay the most attention to:

✔ **Company location:** Stocks and the companies that issue them are classified based on the location of their main operations and headquarters. Funds that specialize in U.S. stocks are, not surprisingly, called U.S. stock funds; those that focus overseas typically are called international or overseas funds.

✔ **Growth stocks versus value stocks:** Stock fund managers and their funds are categorized by whether they invest in growth or value stocks.

- *Growth stocks* have high prices in relation to the company's assets, profits, and potential profits. Growth companies typically experience rapidly expanding revenue and profits. These companies tend to reinvest most of their earnings in the company to fuel future expansion; thus, these stocks pay no or low dividends.

- *Value stocks* are priced cheaply in relation to the company's assets, profits, and potential profits. Value stocks tend to pay higher dividends than growth stocks and historically have produced higher total returns.

✔ **Company size:** Another dimension on which a stock fund's stock selection differs is based on the size of the company in which the fund invests: small, medium, or large. The total market value — *capitalization,* or *cap* for short — of a company's outstanding stock defines the categories of the stocks that the fund invests in. Small-capitalization stocks are usually defined as stocks of companies that possess total market capitalization of less than $2 billion. Medium-capitalization stocks have market values of $2 billion to $10 billion. Large-capitalization stocks are those of companies with market values greater than $10 billion. (***Note:*** These definitions can change over time.)

Putting together two or three of these major classifications, you can start to comprehend those lengthy names that are given to stock funds. You can have funds that focus on large-company value stocks or small-company growth stocks. You can add U.S., international, and worldwide funds to further subdivide these categories into more fund types. So you can have international stock funds that focus on small-company stocks or growth stocks.

You can purchase several stock funds, each focusing on a different type of stock, to diversify into various types of stocks. Two potential advantages result from doing so:

✔ Not all your money rides in one stock fund and with one fund manager.

✔ Each of the different fund managers can look at and track particular stock investment possibilities.

The following sections describe the best stock funds that are worthy of your consideration.

U.S. stock funds

Of all the types of funds offered, U.S. stock funds are the largest category. The only way to know for sure where a fund currently invests (or where the fund may invest in the future) is to ask. You can call the mutual fund company that you're interested in to start your information search, or you can visit the company's website. You can also read the fund's annual report. (The prospectus generally doesn't tell you what the fund currently invests in or has invested in.)

Here's my short list of U.S. stock funds:

✔ Dodge & Cox Stock (800-621-3979; www.dodgeandcox.com)

✔ Sequoia (800-686-6884; www.sequoiafund.com)

✔ T. Rowe Price Spectrum Growth — actually a global fund that invests in some foreign stocks (800-638-5660; www.troweprice.com)

✔ Vanguard Total Stock Market Index, Primecap, Selected Value, Tax-Managed Capital Appreciation, and Tax-Managed Small Capitalization (800-662-7447; www.vanguard.com)

International stock funds

Be sure to invest in stock funds that invest overseas for diversification and growth potential. You usually can tell that you're looking at a fund that focuses its investments overseas if its name contains the word *International,* which typically means that the fund's stock holdings are foreign only. If the fund name includes the word *Global* or *Worldwide,* the fund holds both foreign and U.S. stocks.

Shun foreign funds that invest in just one country. As with investing in a sector fund that specializes in a particular industry, this lack of diversification defeats a major benefit of investing in funds. Funds that focus on specific regions, such as Southeast Asia, are better but generally still problematic because of poor diversification and higher expenses than those of other, more-diversified international funds.

If you want to invest in more geographically limiting international funds, take a look at T. Rowe Price's and Vanguard's offerings, which invest in broader regions, such as investing just in Europe, Asia, and the volatile but higher-growth-potential emerging markets in Southeast Asia and Latin America.

In addition to the risks normally inherent with stock fund investing, changes in the value of foreign currencies relative to the U.S. dollar cause price changes in international stocks. A decline in the value of the U.S. dollar helps the value of foreign stock funds. Conversely, a rising dollar versus other currencies can reduce the value of foreign stocks. Some foreign stock funds hedge against currency changes. Although this hedging helps reduce volatility, it does cost money.

Here are my picks for diversified international funds:

- ✔ Dodge & Cox International (800-621-3979; www.dodgeandcox.com)

- ✔ Harbor International (800-422-1050; www.harborfunds.com)

- ✔ Litman Gregory Masters' International (800-960-0188; www.mastersfunds.com)

- ✔ Oakmark International and Global — holds some U.S. stocks (800-625-6275; www.oakmark.com)

- ✔ Tweedy, Browne Global Value — invests in the United States as well (800-432-4789; www.tweedybrowne.com)

- ✔ Vanguard Global Equity (invests in the United States too), International Growth, Tax-Managed International, and Total International Stock Index (800-662-7447; www.vanguard.com)

Balancing your act: Funds that combine stocks and bonds

Some funds — generally known as *balanced funds* — invest in both bonds and stocks. These funds are usually less risky and less volatile than funds that invest exclusively in stocks. In an economic downturn, bonds usually hold value better than stocks do.

Balanced funds make it easier for investors who are skittish about investing in stocks to hold stocks because they reduce the volatility that normally comes with pure stock funds. Because of their extensive diversification, balanced funds are also excellent choices for an investor who doesn't have much money to start with.

Balanced funds aren't appropriate for some investors who purchase funds outside tax-sheltered retirement accounts because these funds pay decent dividends from the bonds that they hold. With the exception of the Vanguard Tax-Managed Balanced Fund, which holds federal-tax-free bonds, you should avoid balanced funds if you're in a higher tax bracket. Consider buying separate tax-friendly stock funds and tax-free bond funds to create your own balanced portfolio.

Here's my short list of great balanced funds:

- ✔ Dodge & Cox Balanced (800-621-3979; www.dodgeand-cox.com)

- ✔ Fidelity Freedom Funds and Fidelity Puritan (800-343-3548; www.fidelity.com)

- ✔ T. Rowe Price Balanced (800-638-5660; www.troweprice.com)

- ✔ Vanguard LifeStrategy Funds, Wellesley Income, and Wellington (800-662-7447; www.vanguard.com)

Finding the best bond funds

Although there are thousands of bond fund choices, not many remain after you eliminate high-cost funds, low-performance funds, and funds managed by fund companies and fund managers with minimal experience investing in bonds (all key points that I address in "Maximizing Your Chances for Fund Investing Success," earlier in this chapter).

Among the key considerations when choosing bond funds are

- ✔ **Years to maturity:** Bond-fund objectives and names usually fit one of three maturity categories: short-, intermediate-, and long-term. You can generally earn a higher yield from investing in a bond fund that holds longer-term bonds, but such bond prices are more sensitive to changes in interest rates. (*Duration,* which quantifies a bond fund's sensitivity to changes in interest rates, is another term you may come across. A fund with a duration of eight years means that if interest rates rise by 1 percent, the fund should decline by 8 percent.)

- ✔ **Bond credit quality:** The lower the issuer's credit rating, the riskier the bond. As with the risk associated with longer maturities, a fund that holds lower-quality bonds should provide higher returns for the increased risk you take. A higher yield is the bond market's way of compensating you for taking greater risk. Funds holding higher-quality bonds provide lower returns but more security.

- ✔ **Fees and costs:** After you settle on the type of bonds that you want, you must consider a bond fund's costs, including its sales commissions and annual operating fees. Stick with no-load funds that maintain lower annual operating expenses.

- ✔ **Taxability:** Pay attention to the taxability of the dividends that bonds pay. If you're investing in bonds inside retirement accounts, you want taxable bonds. If you invest in bonds outside retirement accounts, the choice between taxable and tax-free depends on your tax bracket.

- ✔ **Type of bond issuer:** Bonds can be issued by corporations, state and local governments, the federal government, and foreign entities (corporate and governments). Although some bond funds hold an eclectic mix, many focus on specific types of bonds (such as corporate bonds).

Because bond funds fluctuate in value, invest in them only if you have sufficient money in an emergency reserve. If you invest money for longer-term purposes, particularly retirement, you need to come up with an overall plan for allocating your money among a variety of funds, including bond funds.

The dangers of yield-chasing

When selecting bond funds to invest in, investors are often led astray as to how much they can expect to make. The first mistake is looking at recent performance and assuming that you'll get that return in the future.

Investing in bond funds based on recent performance is particularly tempting immediately after a period where interest rates have declined, because declines in interest rates pump up bond prices and, therefore, bond funds' total returns. Remember that an equal but opposite force waits to counteract high bond returns as bond prices fall when interest rates rise.

To make performance numbers meaningful and useful, you must compare bond funds that are comparable, such as intermediate-term funds that invest exclusively in high-grade corporate bonds.

Bond funds calculate their yield after subtracting their operating expenses. When you contact a fund company seeking a fund's current yield, make sure that you understand what time period the yield covers. Fund companies are supposed to give you the Securities and Exchange Commission (SEC) yield, which is a standard yield calculation that allows for fairer comparisons among bond funds. The SEC yield, which reflects the bond fund's yield to maturity, is the best yield to use when you compare funds because it captures the effective rate of interest that an investor can receive in the future.

If you select bond funds based on advertised yield, you're quite likely to purchase the wrong bond funds. Bond funds and the fund companies that sell them can play more than a few games to fatten a fund's yield. Higher yields make it easier for salespeople and funds to hawk their bond funds. Remember that yield-enhancing shenanigans can leave you poorer. Here's what you need to watch out for:

✔ **Lower-credit-quality bonds:** When comparing one bond fund with another, you may discover that one pays a higher yield and decide that it looks better. You may find out later, however, that the higher-yielding fund invests a sizeable chunk of its money in junk (non-investment-grade) bonds, whereas the other fund fully invests only in high-quality bonds.

✔ **Longer-maturity bonds:** Bond funds usually can increase their yield just by increasing their maturity a bit. So if one short-term bond fund invests in bonds that mature in an average of two years, and another fund has an average maturity of seven years, comparing the two is comparing apples and oranges.

✔ **Return of principal as dividends:** Some funds return a portion of your principal in the form of dividends. This move artificially pumps up a fund's yield but actually depresses its total return. When you compare bond funds, make sure that you compare their total return over time in addition to making sure that they have comparable portfolios of bonds.

✔ **Temporary waivers of expenses:** Some bond funds, particularly newer ones, waive a portion or even all of their operating expenses to inflate the fund's yield temporarily. Bond funds that engage in this practice often quietly end their expense waiver when the bond market is performing well.

Recommended short-term bond funds

Short-term bonds work well for money that you earmark for use in a few years, such as to purchase a home or a car, and for money that you plan to withdraw from your retirement account in the near future.

Short-term bond funds are the least sensitive to interest rate fluctuations in the bond-fund universe. The stability of short-term bond funds makes them appropriate investments for money on which you seek a better rate of return than a money market fund can produce for you. With short-term bond funds, however, you also have to tolerate the risk of losing a percentage or two in principal value if interest rates rise.

Consider bond funds that pay taxable dividends when you're not in a high tax bracket and when you want to invest inside retirement accounts. My favorite is the Vanguard Short-Term Investment-Grade fund.

U.S. Treasury bond funds may be appropriate if you prefer a bond fund that invests in U.S. Treasuries, which possess the safety of government backing. They're also a fine choice if you're not in a high federal tax bracket but are in a high state tax bracket (5 percent or higher). Vanguard Short-Term

Treasury is a good choice. I don't recommend Treasuries for retirement accounts because they pay less interest than fully taxable bond funds.

State- and federal-tax-free short-term bond funds are scarce. If you want short-term bonds, and if you're in a high federal tax bracket but in a low state tax bracket (less than 5 percent), consider investing in these federal-tax-free bond funds (whose dividends are state-taxable):

- ✔ Vanguard Short-Term Tax-Exempt (800-662-7447; www. vanguard.com)

- ✔ Vanguard Limited-Term Tax-Exempt (800-662-7447; www. vanguard.com)

If you live in a state with high taxes, consider checking out the state- and federal-tax-free intermediate-term bond funds (which I discuss in the next section) if you can withstand their volatility.

Recommended intermediate-term bond funds

Intermediate-term bond funds hold bonds that typically mature in a decade or so. They're more volatile than shorter-term bonds but can also be more rewarding. The longer you own an intermediate-term bond fund, the more likely you are to earn a higher return on it than on a short-term fund unless interest rates continue to rise over many years.

As an absolute minimum, don't purchase an intermediate-term fund unless you expect to hold it for three to five years — or even longer, if you can. Therefore, you need to make sure that the money you put in an immediate-term fund is money that you don't expect to use in the near future.

Taxable intermediate-term bond funds to consider include the following:

- ✔ Dodge & Cox Income (800-621-3979; www.dodgeandcox. com)

- ✔ Harbor Bond (800-422-1050; www.harborfunds.com)

- ✔ Vanguard Total Bond Market Index (800-662-7447; www. vanguard.com)

Consider U.S. Treasury bond funds if you prefer a bond fund that invests in U.S. Treasuries, which provide the safety of government backing. You can also invest in them if you're not in a high federal tax bracket but are in a high state tax bracket (5 percent or higher). A couple of my favorites are Vanguard Inflation-Protected Securities and Vanguard Intermediate-Term Treasury. I don't recommend Treasuries for retirement accounts because they pay less interest than fully taxable bond funds.

Consider federal-tax-free bond funds if you're in a high federal tax bracket but a relatively low state tax bracket (less than 5 percent). Good ones include

✔ Fidelity Intermediate Municipal Income (800-343-3548; www.fidelity.com)

✔ Vanguard Intermediate-Term Tax-Exempt (800-662-7447; www.vanguard.com)

If you're in high federal and state tax brackets, refer to the state- and federal-tax-free bond fund company providers that I mention in the next section.

Recommended long-term bond funds

Long-term bond funds are the most aggressive and volatile bond funds around. If interest rates on long-term bonds increase substantially, you can easily see the principal value of your investment decline 10 percent or more.

Long-term bond funds are generally used for retirement investing in one of two situations by investors who

✔ Don't expect to tap their investment money for a decade or more

✔ Want to maximize current dividend income and are willing to tolerate volatility

Don't use long-term bond funds to invest money that you plan to use within the next five years, because a bond-market drop can leave your portfolio short of your monetary goal.

I have just one favorite taxable bond fund that holds longer-term bonds: the Vanguard Long-Term Investment-Grade fund (800-662-7447; www.vanguard.com).

U.S. Treasury bond funds may be advantageous if you want a bond fund that invests in U.S. Treasuries. They're also great if you're not in a high federal tax bracket but are in a high state tax bracket (5 percent or higher). I recommend Treasuries for non-retirement accounts only because Treasuries pay less interest than fully taxable bond funds. I recommend the Vanguard Long-Term Treasury fund (800-662-7447; www. vanguard.com).

State and federally tax-free bond funds may be appropriate when you're in high federal and state (5 percent or higher) tax brackets. A municipal (federal-tax-free) long-term bond fund that I recommend is Vanguard Long-Term Tax-Exempt. Fidelity, T. Rowe Price, and Vanguard offer good funds for several states. If you can't find a good state-specific fund where you live, or if you're in a high federal tax bracket, you can use the nationwide Vanguard Municipal bond funds.

Considering Alternatives to Investing in Funds

If you're getting into the investment game, you'll likely hear about, and be pitched, some alternatives to investing in funds. In this section, I reveal the truth about those options.

Your own online fund

On some websites, various services claim that you can invest in a chosen basket of stocks for a low fee and without the high taxes and high fees that come with mutual fund investing.

These "create your own funds" services pitch their investment products as superior alternatives to mutual funds. One such service calls its investment vehicles *folios,* charging you $29 per month ($290 per year paid in advance) to invest in folios, each of which can hold a few dozen stocks that are selected from the universe of stocks that this service makes available. The fee covers trading in your folios that may occur only during two time windows each day that the stock market is open. Thus, in addition to the burden of managing your own portfolio of stocks, you have virtually no control of the timing of your trades during the trading day.

According to my analysis, you'd need to invest more than $150,000 through this folio service to come out ahead in terms of the explicit fees. You also need to be aware of additional fees, which you usually have to search the fine print to find. You may get whacked $30 to wire money out of your account or even $50 to close an account!

Evaluating the performance of self-created funds is difficult. Also, unlike mutual funds, these funds have no standards or easily accessible services that report and track the performance of your customized folio.

Unit investment trusts

Unit investment trusts (UITs) have much in common with both mutual funds and exchange-traded funds. UITs take a fixed initial amount of money and buy securities that meet the objectives of the UIT. Unlike a mutual fund, however, a UIT doesn't make any changes in its holdings over time. This holding of a diversified portfolio can be advantageous because it reduces trading costs and possible tax bills.

With that said, UITs do suffer from the following major flaws:

- **High commissions:** Brokers like to sell UITs for the same reason that they like to pitch load mutual funds: the commissions paid out of your investment. Commissions usually are around 5 percent, so for every $10,000 that you invest in a UIT, $500 comes out of your investment and goes into the broker's pocket. (Although UITs do have ongoing fees, their fees tend to be lower than those of most actively managed mutual funds — typically, in the neighborhood of 0.2 percent per year. The best no-load funds also have reasonable management fees, and some charge even less than UITs charge.)

- **Lack of liquidity:** Especially in the first few years after a particular UIT is issued, you won't readily find an active market in which you can easily sell your UIT. In the event that you can find someone who's interested in buying a UIT that you're interested in selling, you'll likely have to sell the UIT at a discount from its actual market value at the time.

> ✔ **Lack of ongoing management oversight:** Because UITs
> buy and hold a fixed set of securities until the UITs are
> liquidated (years down the road), they're more likely to
> get stuck holding some securities that end up worthless.
> Compared with the best bond funds, bond UITs are more
> likely to end up holding bonds in companies that go
> bankrupt.

Brokerage managed accounts

Brokerage firms offer investment management services for
an ongoing fee rather than commissions. (Merrill Lynch is
one common example of a brokerage firm.) *Wrap accounts,* or
managed accounts, go by a variety of names, but they're the
same in one crucial way: For the privilege of investing your
money through their chosen money managers, they charge
you a percentage of the assets that they're managing for you.
These accounts are quite similar to mutual funds except that
the accounts don't have the same regulatory and reporting
requirements.

These managed accounts tend to have relatively high fees —
upward of 2 percent per year of assets under management.
No-load mutual funds and ETFs offer investors access to the
nation's best investment managers for a fraction of the cost of
brokerage managed accounts. Many excellent funds are available for 0.5 percent or less annually.

Hedge funds for the wealthier

Hedge funds, historically investments reserved for big-ticket
investors, seem to be like mutual funds in that they typically
invest in stocks and bonds. They have the added glamour and
allure, however, of taking significant risks and gambles with
their investments. Here's how they stack up compared with
mutual funds and ETFs:

> ✔ **Hedge funds are often much higher-risk.** When a hedge
> fund manager bets right, he can produce high returns.
> When he doesn't, however, his fund can get clobbered.
> With short selling, because the value of the security that
> was sold short can rise an unlimited amount, the poten-
> tial loss from buying it back at a much higher price can

be horrendous. Hedge fund managers have also been clobbered when a previously fast-rising commodity, such as natural gas or copper futures, plunges in value or an investment they make with leverage goes the wrong direction. Several hedge funds went belly-up when their managers guessed wrong. In other words, their investments did so poorly that investors in the fund lost everything. This won't occur with a mutual fund or an ETF.

✔ **Hedge funds have much higher fees.** Hedge funds charge an annual management fee of about 1 percent to 2 percent and a performance fee, which typically amounts to a whopping 20 percent of a fund's profits.

✔ **Hedge funds have had problems with fraud and lousy returns.** During the severe stock market decline in the late 2000s, many hedge funds did poorly. Some funds went under or were exposed to be Ponzi schemes, the most notorious being the fund run by the now-jailed Bernie Madoff. According to *Forbes* magazine, "Hedge funds exist in a lawless and risky realm. . . . Hedge funds aren't even required to keep audited books — and many don't." They're often "guilty of inadequate disclosure of costs, overvaluation of holdings to goose reported performance and manager pay, and cozy ties between funds and brokers that often shortchange investors." Objective studies of all hedge fund returns show that they underperform funds, which makes sense, because hedge funds have the burden of much higher fees.

Part IV
Advanced
Investments

The 5th Wave   By Rich Tennant

"Robert wants to use a traditional method of financing our real estate investments known as OPM — Other People-in-laws Money."

In this part...

1 cover more-complicated but often-rewarding investments in these chapters. First up is real estate, starting
with a home in which you live and then moving along to real
estate you own and rent out. I also discuss investments you
can make in small business, including starting your own
small business and buying or investing in someone else's.
In the last chapter, I delve into some less-conventional but
popular investments, including annuities, life insurance,
gold and other commodities, and collectibles.

Chapter 11

Seeking Shelter and Appreciation in Real Estate

*T*hinking of a home in which you live as an investment may seem like a poor idea to you. In many parts of the country, home prices suffered in the late 2000s and early 2010s.

But although homes may require plenty of financial feeding, over the course of your adult years, owning rather than renting a home can make and save you money. Although the pile of mortgage debt seems daunting in the years just after your purchase, someday your home may be among your biggest assets.

Like stocks, real estate does well over the long term but doesn't go continuously higher. Astute investors take advantage of down periods; they consider these periods to be times to buy at lower prices, just as they do when their favorite retail stores are having a sale.

Comparing Owning a Home to Renting

As financial decisions go, deciding whether and when to buy a home is pretty challenging. You have plenty of financial considerations to contend with, as well as personal issues. Psychologically, many folks equate buying a home with settling down. After all, you'll be coming home to your home day after day, year after year. You can always move, of course, but doing so can be costly and time-consuming, and as a home-owner, you'll have a financial obligation to deal with.

In this section, I cover the important issues to consider when comparing buying to renting.

Weighing financial considerations

You've probably already heard some arguments regarding the supposed financial benefits of owning a home. These benefits include the notion of buying and owning a home for the tax breaks, as well as the thought that paying rent is analogous to throwing your money away.

The biggest homeownership costs are mortgage interest and property taxes, and in the United States, these costs are generally tax-deductible. The tax breaks are already largely factored into the higher cost of owning a home, however, so you should never buy a home just because of the tax breaks.

Renting isn't necessarily like throwing your money away. In fact, renting can have several benefits, including the following:

- ✔ **Renting sometimes costs less (sometimes much less) than owning.** In the mid-2000s, in some parts of the country, renting a given property cost about half as much as owning that same property (a monthly comparison even after factoring in the tax benefits of owning).

- ✔ **You may be able to save more toward your personal and financial goals if you can rent at a relatively low cost.** You can invest, for example, in other financial assets such as stocks, bonds, and funds (and may be able to do so through tax-favored accounts).

- ✔ **Renting has potential emotional and psychological rewards.** You usually have more flexibility to pack up and move on as a renter. You may have a lease to fulfill, but you may be able to renegotiate it if circumstances require you to move. As a homeowner, you have some major monthly payments to take care of. To some people, this responsibility feels like a financial ball and chain. After all, you have no guarantee that you can sell your home in a timely fashion or at the price you desire if you want or need to move.

Renting does have at least one big drawback: exposure to inflation (cost-of-living increases). As the cost of living increases, unless you live in a rent-controlled unit, your landlord can keep increasing your rent. By contrast, if you're a homeowner, your largest monthly expense — the mortgage payment — doesn't increase, assuming that you buy your home with a fixed-rate mortgage. Your property taxes, homeowner's insurance, and maintenance expenses are exposed to inflation, but these expenses are usually much smaller in comparison with your monthly mortgage payment.

Considering costs and your time frame

You face significant costs when buying and selling a home. My analysis suggests that you probably need at least five years of low appreciation to recoup your transaction costs. Some of the expenses you face when buying and selling a home include the following:

- ✓ **Agent's commission:** Real estate agents generally charge a commission of 5 percent to 7 percent of the purchase price. Even if the seller is technically paying the commission out of the proceeds that he or she receives from selling a home, both the buyer and seller of a home are effectively paying commissions because those costs are built into the home's sale price. (You may be able to reduce these costs by doing the selling yourself, but a buyer may offer less, knowing that you're not having to pay commission.)

- ✓ **Inspection fees:** When you buy a property, you should hire a professional to thoroughly check it out. Good inspectors can help you identify problems with the plumbing, heating, electrical systems, foundation, roof, pests like termites, and so on. Property inspections typically cost at least a few hundred dollars up to $1,000 for larger homes.

- ✓ **Moving expenses:** Moving costs vary wildly, but you can count on spending hundreds to thousands of dollars. Costs increase with the distance you have to go and the amount of stuff you have, of course.

- ✓ **Mortgage costs:** The costs of getting a mortgage include such items as the *points* (up-front interest — about 1 percent to 2 percent of the loan amount), application and credit report fees, and appraisal fees.

✔ **Title insurance:** When you buy a home, you and your lender will want to protect yourselves against the small probability that the property seller doesn't actually legally own the home that you're buying. Title insurance protects you financially from unscrupulous sellers. Although title insurance costs vary by area, 0.5 percent of the purchase price of the property is about average.

On top of all these transaction costs of buying and then selling a home, you face maintenance expenses — repairs, cosmetic work, and so on — during your years of home ownership. To cover the typical transaction and maintenance costs of home-ownership, the value of your home needs to appreciate about 15 percent over the years that you own it for you to be as well off financially as if you'd continued renting. Counting on that kind of appreciation in case you need or want to move else-where in a few years is risky.

Some people invest in real estate even when they don't expect to live in the home long, and they may consider turning their home into a rental if they move within a few years. Doing so can work well financially in the long haul, but don't underestimate the responsibilities that come with rental property. See the section "Investing in Investment Real Estate," later in this chapter.

Deciding when to buy

If you're considering buying a home, you may be concerned about whether home prices are poised to rise or fall. No one wants to purchase a home that then plummets in value. And who wouldn't like to buy just before prices zoom higher?

It's not easy to predict what's going to happen with real estate prices in a particular town or neighborhood over the next few years. Ultimately, the economic health and vitality of an area drive the demand and prices for homes in that area. An increase in jobs, particularly ones that pay well, increases the demand for housing, and when demand goes up, so do prices.

If you buy your first home when you're in your 20s or 30s, you will likely be a homeowner for many decades. Over such a long time, you will surely experience numerous ups and downs. But you'll probably see more ups than downs, so don't be too concerned about trying to predict what's going to happen to the real estate market in the near term and whether prices may fall a little. You should do a basic rent-versus-buy comparison, of course, to see whether the properties you're considering offer decent value or not. A silver lining of the late-2000s decline in home prices is that homes are now more affordable than they have been in a long time and offer good value versus renting in many areas.

That said, at particular times in your life, you may be ambivalent about buying a home. Perhaps you're not sure whether you'll stay put for five years. Therefore, part of your home-buying decision may hinge on whether current home prices versus the costs of renting in your local area offer you a good value. The state of the job market, the number of home listings for sale, and the level of real estate prices compared with rent are useful indicators of the housing market's health.

 Trying to time your purchase has more importance if you think you may move within a few years. In that case, avoid buying in a market where home prices are relatively high compared with rental costs. If you expect to move so soon, renting generally makes sense because of the high transaction costs of buying and selling real estate.

Figuring Your Home-Buying Budget

Buying a home is a long-term financial commitment. You'll probably take out a 15- or 30-year mortgage to finance your purchase, and the home you buy will need maintenance over time. So before you decide to buy, take stock of your overall financial health, determine how large a down payment you'll need, and understand how much lenders will be willing to lend you.

Getting your financial house in order

To qualify for a mortgage, you need good credit and a stable, reliable source of employment income. Mortgage lenders will tell you the maximum amount that you're qualified to borrow. Just because they offer you that maximum amount, however, doesn't mean that you should borrow that much.

Buying a home without considering your other monthly expenditures and long-term goals may cause you to end up with a home that dictates much of your future spending. Have you considered, for example, how much you need to save monthly to reach your goals? How about the amount you want to spend on your current lifestyle?

If you want to continue your current lifestyle, you have to be honest with yourself about how much you can really afford to spend as a homeowner. First-time home buyers in particular run into financial trouble when they don't understand their current spending.

Buying a home can be a wise decision, but it can also be a huge burden. Also, you can buy all sorts of nifty things for a home. Some people prop up their spending habits with credit cards — a dangerous practice. So before you buy a property or agree to a particular mortgage, be sure that you can afford to do so and that it fits with your overall plans and desires.

Determining your down payment

When deciding how much to borrow for a home purchase, keep in mind that most lenders require you to purchase private mortgage insurance (PMI) if your down payment is less than 20 percent of your home's purchase price. PMI protects the lender from getting stuck with a property that may be worth less than the mortgage you owe, in the event that you default on your loan. On a moderate-size loan, PMI can add hundreds of dollars per year to your payments.

If you have to purchase PMI to buy a home with less than 20 percent down, keep an eye on your home's value and your loan balance. Over time, your property should appreciate, and your loan balance should decrease as you make monthly payments. After your mortgage represents 80 percent or less of the market value of the home, you can get rid of the PMI. Doing so usually entails contacting your lender and paying for an appraisal.

I've never liked interest-only loans, which entice cash-strapped buyers with lower monthly payments because all the initial payments go toward interest. These loans typically have higher interest rates and fees than conventional mortgages do, and they cause some buyers to take on more debt than they can handle. (After a certain number of years, the payment amount jumps higher when the principal and interest begin to be repaid together.)

What if you can afford to make more than a 20 percent down payment? How much should you put down then? (This problem is rare; most buyers, especially first-time buyers, struggle to get a 20 percent down payment together.) The answer depends on what else you can or want to do with the money. If you're considering other investment opportunities, determine whether you can expect to earn a higher rate of return on those other investments versus the interest rate that you'd pay on the mortgage. (Forget about the tax deduction for your mortgage interest. The interest is deductible, but remember that the earnings from your investments are ultimately taxable.)

All investments come with risk. If you prefer to put down just 20 percent and invest more money elsewhere, that's fine. Just don't keep the extra money (beyond an emergency reserve) under the mattress, in a savings account, or in bonds with a lower yield than your mortgage's interest rate. Invest in stocks, real estate, or other growth investments. Otherwise, you don't have a chance of earning a higher return than the cost of your mortgage; therefore, you'd be better off paying down your mortgage.

Doing lenders' calculations

Mortgage lenders calculate the maximum amount that you can borrow to buy a home. All lenders want to gauge your ability to repay the money that you borrow, so you have to pass a few tests.

For a home in which you will live, lenders total your monthly housing expenses. They define your housing costs as

Mortgage payment + Property taxes + Insurance

Note: Lenders don't consider maintenance and upkeep expenses (including utilities) in owning a home, but of course, you will incur these expenses as a homeowner.

Assessing consumer debt

Although lenders may not care where you spend money outside your home, they do care about your other debt. A lot of other debt, such as consumer debt on credit cards or auto loans, diminishes the funds that are available to pay your housing expenses. Lenders know that having other debt increases the possibility that you may fall behind or actually default on your mortgage payments.

If you have consumer debt that requires monthly payments, lenders calculate another ratio to determine the maximum that you can borrow for a home. Lenders add the amount that you need to pay on your other consumer debt to your monthly housing expense.

Consumer debt is bad news, even without considering the fact that it hurts your qualification for a mortgage. This type of debt is costly and encourages you to live beyond your means. Unlike the interest on mortgage debt, consumer debt interest isn't tax-deductible.

Get rid of your consumer debt as soon as possible. Curtail your spending, and adjust to living within your means. If you can't live within your means as a renter, you won't be able to do it as a homeowner either.

Determining homeownership tax savings

Your mortgage interest and property taxes are generally tax-deductible on Form 1040, Schedule A of your personal tax return. When you calculate the costs of owning a home, subtract the tax savings to get a more complete and accurate sense of what homeownership will cost you.

When you finally buy a home, refigure how much you need to pay in income tax, because your mortgage interest and property tax deductions can help lower your income tax bill. If you work for an employer, ask your payroll/benefits department for Form W-4. If you're self-employed, you can complete a worksheet that comes with Form 1040-ES. (Call 800-829-3676 for a copy.) Many new home buyers don't bother with this step, and they receive a big tax refund on their next filed income tax return. Although getting money back from the Internal Revenue Service may feel good, it means that at minimum, you gave the IRS an interest-free loan. In the worst-case scenario, the reduced cash flow during the year may cause you to accumulate other debt or miss out on contributing to tax-deductible retirement accounts.

If you want a more precise estimate of how home ownership may affect your tax situation, get out your tax return, and plug in some reasonable numbers to guesstimate how your taxes may change. You can also speak with a tax advisor.

Down the road, also know that eligible homeowners can exclude a large portion of their gain on the sale of a principal residence from taxable income: up to $250,000 for single tax-payers and up to $500,000 for married couples filing jointly.

Shopping for Your Home

Be realistic about how long it may take you to get up to speed about different areas and to find a home that meets your various desires. If you're like most people, with a full-time job that allows only occasional evenings and weekends free to look for a house, three to six months is a short period to settle on an area and actually find and successfully negotiate for a property. Six months to a year isn't unusual or slow.

Remember that you're talking about an enormous purchase that you'll come home to daily. Buying a home can also involve a lot of compromise when you buy with other family members, particularly spouses.

Real estate agents can be a big barrier to taking your time with this monumental decision. Some agents are pushy; they just want to make a sale and get their commission. Don't work with such agents as a buyer, because they can make you stressed and broke. If necessary, begin your search without an agent to avoid this outside pressure.

In this section, I discuss your housing choices, how to research communities, and finally how to check out homes and value them.

Understanding your housing options

If you're ready to buy a home, to help focus your search, you should make some decisions about what and where to buy. Here are the most common types of housing you will encounter:

- ✔ **Single-family homes:** If you grew up in the suburbs, you probably saw plenty of single-family homes, even if you didn't live in one. This type of home is a detached house on a piece of land. Lots may be small or large, but the land is 100 percent yours, and the house is separate from other neighboring properties.

- ✔ **Condominiums:** These properties typically are apartment-style units that are on top of and adjacent to one another. Many condo buildings were originally apartments that were converted to condos through the sale of ownership of separate units. When you purchase a condominium, you purchase a specific unit as well as a share of the common areas (the pool, landscaping, entry and hallways, laundry room, and so on).

- ✔ **Townhomes:** Townhomes are attached or row homes. A townhome is essentially a cross between a condominium (because it's attached, sharing a roof and some walls) and a single-family house (because it has its own yard).

- ✔ **Cooperatives:** Cooperatives (or co-ops) resemble apartment and condominium buildings. When you buy a share in a cooperative, you own a share of the entire building, including some living space. Unlike in a condo, you generally need to get approval from the cooperative association if you want to remodel or rent your unit to a tenant. In some co-ops, you must even gain approval from the association to sell your unit to a proposed buyer.

Co-ops generally are much harder to obtain loans for and to sell, so I don't recommend that you buy one unless you get a good deal and can obtain a loan easily.

With the exception of single-family homes in the preceding list, the other types of housing are shared housing. This type of housing generally gives you more living space for your dollars. This value makes sense, because a good chunk of the cost of a single-family home is the land on which the home sits. Land is good for decks, recreation, and children's playgrounds, but you don't live "in" land the way you do in your home. Shared housing maximizes living space for the housing dollars that you spend.

Another possible benefit of shared housing is that in many situations, you're not personally responsible for general maintenance. Instead, the homeowners' association (which you pay into) takes care of it. If you don't have the time, energy, or desire to keep up a property, shared housing can make sense.

Shared housing units may also give you access to recreation facilities, such as a pool, tennis courts, and exercise equipment.

From an investment perspective, shared housing isn't best. Single-family homes generally appreciate more than shared housing does. Part of the reason for that is that shared housing is easier to build and to overbuild, and the greater supply tends to keep prices from rising as much. On the demand side, single-family homes tend to attract more potential buyers. Most folks, when they can afford it, prefer a stand-alone home, especially for the increased privacy.

If you can afford a smaller single-family home instead of a larger shared-housing unit and don't balk at maintaining a home, buy a single-family home. Shared housing makes more sense for people who don't want to deal with maintenance and who value the security of living in a larger building with other folks. Shared-housing prices tend to hold up better in developed urban environments. If possible, avoid shared housing units in suburban areas, where the availability of developable land makes building many more units possible, thus increasing the supply of housing and slowing growth in value.

Researching communities

You may have an idea about the type of property and location that interests you or that you think you can afford. Even if you've lived in an area for a while and think that you know it well, be sure to explore different types of properties in a variety of locations before you start to narrow your search.

Thinking that you can know what an area is like from anecdotes or from a small number of personal experiences is a mistake. Anecdotes and people's perceptions often aren't accurate reflections of the facts. Check out the following key items in an area you're considering:

> ✔ **Amenities:** Ideally, you don't spend all your time at work, slaving away to make your monthly mortgage payment. I hope that you have time to use parks, sports and recreation facilities, and so on. Walk and drive around the neighborhoods you're interested in to get a sense of these attractions. Most real estate agents enjoy showing their favorite neighborhoods. Talk to folks you know in the areas you're considering. Visit those cities' and towns' websites.

✔ **Catastrophic risks:** Are the neighborhoods in which you're considering buying a home prone to floods, tornadoes, mudslides, fires, or earthquakes? Although homeowner's insurance, with proper supplements, can protect you financially, consider how you may deal with such catastrophes emotionally. Insurance addresses only the financial pain of a home loss. You can't eliminate all risks, but you can get educated about catastrophic risks. The U.S. Geological Survey (www.usgs.gov) has maps that show earthquake risks, and the Federal Emergency Management Agency (www.fema.gov) has flood-risk maps. Insurance companies and agencies can also tell you what they know about risks in particular areas.

✔ **Crime:** Cities and towns keep all sorts of crime statistics for neighborhoods, so use them! Call the local police department, or get local crime data online at sites like www.neighborhoodscout.com.

✔ **Development:** Check with the planning office in towns that you're considering living in to find out what types of new developments and major renovations are in the works. Planning people may also be aware of problems in particular areas.

✔ **Property taxes:** What will your property taxes be? Property tax rates vary from community to community. Check with the town's assessment office or with a good real estate agent.

✔ **Schools:** If you have kids, you care about this issue a lot. Unfortunately, many people make snap judgments about school quality without getting the facts. Visit schools, talk to parents and teachers, and discover what goes on at the schools.

Consider school quality even if schools aren't important to you, because they can affect the resale value of your property.

Checking out and valuing a home

Over many months, you may see dozens of homes for sale. Use these viewings as an opportunity to find out what specific homes are worth. Odds are that the listing price isn't what a house is actually worth. Property that's priced to sell usually does sell. Properties left on the market are often overpriced. The listing prices of such properties may reflect what an otherwise greedy or uninformed seller and his or her agent hope that some fool will pay.

Of the properties that you see, keep track of the prices that they end up selling for. (Good agents can provide this information.) Properties usually sell for less than the listed price. Keeping track of selling prices gives you a good handle on what properties are really worth and a better sense of what you can afford.

After you set your sights on a home you like, thoroughly check out the surroundings. Go back to the neighborhood in which the property is located at different times of the day and on different days of the week. Knock on some doors, and meet your potential neighbors. Ask questions. Talk to property owners as well as renters. Because they don't have a financial stake in the area, renters are often more forthcoming with negative information about an area.

After you decide where and what to buy, you're ready to try to put a deal together. To do so, you need to understand mortgages, negotiations, and inspections. I cover these issues and many more in *Home Buying Kit For Dummies,* 5th Edition (Wiley), which I cowrote with Ray Brown.

Investing in Investment Real Estate

If you've already bought your own home (and even if you haven't), using real estate as an investment may interest you. Real estate investing, like the stock market and small-business investments, has long generated tremendous wealth for many investors.

Real estate is like other types of ownership investments, such as stocks, in that you have an ownership stake in an asset. Although you have the potential for significant profits, don't forget that you also accept greater risk. Like stocks, real estate goes through good and bad performance periods. Most people who make money investing in real estate do so because they invest in and hold property over many years.

Real estate investing isn't for everyone. You should avoid real estate investments that involve managing property if you're pressed for time. Buying and owning investment property and being a landlord take a lot of time. If you fail to do your homework before purchasing real estate, you can end up overpaying — or buying a heap of trouble. You can hire a property manager to help with screening and finding good tenants, as well as troubleshooting problems with the building you purchase, but this step costs money and still requires some time involvement. Also, remember that most tenants don't care for a property the same way that property owners do. If every little scratch or carpet stain sends your blood pressure skyward, avoid the stress of being a landlord.

In this section, I discuss how to make wise real estate investments.

Understanding real estate investment's appeal

Many people build their wealth by investing in real estate. Some people focus exclusively on property investments, but many others build their wealth through the companies that they started or through other avenues and then diversify into real estate investments.

Real estate, like all investments, has its pros and cons. Investing in real estate is time-intensive and carries risks. Do it because you enjoy the challenge and because you want to diversify your portfolio. Don't take this route because you seek a get-rich-quick outlet. Here are some of the reasons why people pursue real estate investments:

- **Ability to add value:** Perhaps you can fix up a property or develop it further and raise the rental income and resale value. Through legwork, persistence, and good negotiating skills, you may also be able to make money by purchasing a property below its fair market value.

- **Appreciation and income:** You can make money from investment real estate through appreciation and from income. The appreciation of your properties compounds without taxation during your ownership. You don't pay tax on this profit until you sell your property, and even then, you can roll over your gain into another investment property to avoid paying tax. The federal tax rate on gains from property held more than one year (known as *long-term capital gains*) are taxed a reduced rate (currently, 15 percent). You also seek to rent out your investment property at a profit based on the property's rental income in excess of its expenses (mortgage, property taxes, insurance, maintenance, and so on). Over time, your operating profit, which is subject to ordinary income tax, should rise as you increase your rental prices faster than your expenses.

✔ **Leverage:** Real estate is different from most other investments because you can borrow 75 percent (or more) of the value of the property to buy it. Thus, you can use your down payment of 25 percent of the purchase price to buy, own, and control a much larger investment; this concept is called *leverage*. You hope, of course, that the value of your real estate goes up; if it does, you make money on your original dollars invested as well as on the money that you borrowed. Leverage can also work against you when prices decline.

✔ **Limited land:** There's a limited supply of buildable, desirable land, and as the population grows, demand for land and housing continues to grow. Land and what you can do with it are what make real estate valuable.

✔ **Longer-term focus:** One problem with investing in the stock market is that prices are constantly changing. Because all you need to do is click your computer mouse or dial a toll-free phone number to place your sell or buy order, some stock market investors fall prey to snap, irrational judgments. While the real estate market is constantly changing, short-term, day-to-day, and week-to-week changes are invisible. If prices do decline over months and years, you're much less likely to sell real estate in a panic. Preparing a property for sale and eventually getting it sold take a good deal of time, and this barrier to selling quickly helps you keep your perspective.

Sizing up real estate investment options

If you think you're cut out to be a landlord and are ready for the responsibility of buying, owning, and managing rental real estate, you have numerous real estate investment options to choose among.

Some investors prefer to buy properties, improve them, and then move on. Ideally, however, you should plan to make real estate investments that you hold for many years, perhaps into your retirement years. But what should you buy? Following is my take on various real estate investments.

Real estate investment trusts

Real estate investment trusts (REITs) are entities that generally invest in different types of property, such as shopping centers, apartments, and other rental buildings. For a fee, REIT managers identify and negotiate the purchase of properties that they believe are good investments; then they manage these properties, including handling all tenant relations.

REITs are a good way to invest in real estate if you don't want the hassles and headaches that come with directly owning and managing rental property. You can research and purchase shares in individual REITs, which trade as securities on the major stock exchanges. An even better approach is to buy a mutual fund or exchange-traded fund that invests in a diversified mixture of REITs.

Residential housing

If you're willing to be a landlord, your best bet for real estate investing is to purchase residential property. People always need places to live. Residential housing is easier to understand, purchase, and manage than most other types of property, such as office and retail property. If you're a homeowner, you already have experience locating, purchasing, and maintaining residential property.

The most common residential housing options are single-family homes, condominiums, and townhouses. You can also purchase multiunit buildings. Consider the following issues when you decide what type of property to buy:

  ✔ **Appreciation potential:** Look for property where simple cosmetic and other fixes may allow you to increase rents and increase the market value of the property. Although condos may be easier to maintain, they tend to appreciate less than homes or apartment buildings do, unless the condos are located in a desirable urban area.

  ✔ **Cash flow:** The difference between the rental income that you collect and the expenses that you pay out is known as your *cash flow*. As time goes on, generating a positive cash flow usually gets easier as you pay down your mortgage debt and increase rents.

✔ **Maintenance:** Condominiums are generally the lowest-maintenance properties because most condominium associations deal with issues such as roofing, gardening, and so on for the entire building. Note that as the owner, you're still responsible for maintenance that's needed inside your unit, such as servicing appliances, interior painting, and so on. Be aware, though, that some condo complexes don't allow rentals. With a single-family home or apartment building, you're responsible for all the maintenance. You can hire someone to do the work, but you still have to find the contractors and coordinate, oversee, and pay for the work they do.

✔ **Tenants:** Single-family homes with just one tenant (which could be a family, a couple, or a single person) are simpler to deal with than a multiunit apartment building that requires the management and maintenance of multiple renters and units.

Unless you really want to minimize maintenance responsibilities, avoid condominium investments. Similarly, apartment-building investments are best left to sophisticated investors who like a challenge and can manage more complex properties. Single-family home investments are generally more straightforward for most people. Be sure that you run the numbers on your rental income and expenses to see whether you can afford the negative cash flow that often occurs in the early years of ownership.

Land

If having tenants and maintaining a building is a lot of work, you can consider investing in land. Over time, in areas experiencing economic and building growth and using up available land, land values appreciate well.

Although land doesn't require upkeep and tenants, it does require financial feeding. Investing in land can be problematic for the following reasons:

✔ **Identifying many years in advance which communities will experience rapid population and job growth isn't easy.** Land in those areas that people believe will be the next hot spot already sells at a premium. If property growth doesn't happen, appreciation will dry up.

✔ **Investing in land is a cash drain.** Because it costs money to purchase land, you also have a mortgage payment to make. Mortgage lenders charge higher interest rates on loans to purchase land because they see it as a more speculative investment.

✔ **You don't get depreciation tax write-offs because land isn't depreciable.** You also have property tax payments to meet, as well as other expenses. With land investments, you don't receive income from the property to offset these expenses.

✔ **If you someday decide that you want to develop the property, it can cost a great deal of money.** Obtaining a loan for development is challenging and more expensive (because it's riskier for the lender) than obtaining a loan for a developed property.

If you decide to invest in land, be sure that you meet the following criteria:

✔ **You can afford it.** Tally up the annual carrying costs so you can see what your cash drain may be. What are the financial consequences of this cash outflow? Will you be able to fund your tax-advantaged retirement accounts, for example? If you can't, count the lost tax benefits as another cost of owning land.

✔ **You understand what further improvements the land needs.** Running utility lines, building roads, landscaping, and so on all cost money. If you plan to develop and build on the land that you purchase, research what these things may cost. Remember that improvements almost always cost more than you expect.

✔ **You know its zoning status.** The value of land depends greatly on what you can develop on it, so thoroughly understand the land's zoning status and what you can — and can't — build on it before you buy. Also research the disposition of the planning department and nearby communities. Areas that are antigrowth and antidevelopment are less likely to be good places for you to invest in land, especially if you need permission to do the type of project that you have in mind.

Be aware that zoning can change for the worse. Sometimes, a zoning alteration can reduce what you can develop on a property and, consequently, the property's value.

> ✔ **You've researched the local economic and housing situations.** Buy land in an area that's home to rapidly expanding companies and that has a shortage of housing and developable land.

Commercial real estate

If you're really motivated and willing to roll up your sleeves, you may want to consider commercial real estate investments (such as small office buildings or strip malls). Generally, however, you're better off *not* investing in such real estate, because it's much more complicated than investing in residential real estate. It's also riskier from an investment and tenant-turnover perspective. When tenants move out, new tenants sometimes require extensive and costly improvements.

In addition to considering investing in commercial real estate when your analysis of the local market suggests that it's a good time to buy, consider it when you can use some of the space to run your own small business. Just as owning your home can be more cost-effective than renting over the years, so is owning commercial real estate if you buy at a reasonably good time and hold the property for many years.

So how do you evaluate the state of your local commercial real estate market? Examine the supply-and-demand statistics over recent years. Determine how much space is available for rent and how that number has changed over time. Also discover the vacancy rate, and find out how it has changed in recent years. Finally, investigate the rental rates, usually quoted as a price per square foot. Ask your local commercial property real estate agent for this data or for the local sources where you can find it.

Here's one way to tell that purchasing a commercial property in a certain area is a bad idea: The supply of available space has increased faster than demand, leading to falling rental rates and higher vacancies. A slowing local economy and an increasing unemployment rate also spell trouble for commercial real estate prices. Each market is different, so make sure that you check out the details of your area.

Conducting real estate investing research

In the following sections, I explain what to look for in a community and area where you seek to invest in real estate. Investing in real estate closer to home is best because you're probably more familiar with the local area, allowing you to have an easier time researching and managing the properties.

Assessing employment vitality

Invest in real estate in communities that maintain diverse job bases. If the local economy relies heavily on jobs in a small number of industries, that dependence increases the risk of your real estate investments. The Bureau of Labor Statistics (www.bls.gov) compiles this type of data for metropolitan areas and counties.

Also determine which industries are most heavily represented in the local economy. Areas that have a greater concentration of high-growth industries stand a greater chance of faster price appreciation.

Finally, check out the unemployment situation, and examine how the jobless rate has changed in recent years. Good signs to look for are declining unemployment and increasing job growth. The Bureau of Labor Statistics also tracks this data.

Evaluating the realty market's health

The price of real estate, like the price of anything else, is driven by supply and demand. The smaller the supply and the greater the demand, the higher prices climb. An abundance of land and available credit, however, inevitably leads to overbuilding. When the supply of anything expands at a much faster rate than demand, prices usually fall.

Upward pressure on real estate prices tends to be greatest in areas with little buildable land. In addition to buildable land, consider these important real estate market indicators to gauge the health of a particular market:

✓ **Building permits:** The trend in the number of building permits tells you how the supply of real estate properties may soon change. A long and sustained rise in permits over several years can indicate that the supply of new property may dampen future price appreciation.

✓ **Vacancy rates:** If few rentals are vacant, you can assume that the area has more competition and demand for existing units, which bodes well for future real estate price appreciation. Conversely, high vacancy rates indicate an excess supply of real estate, which may put downward pressure on rental rates as many landlords compete to attract tenants.

✓ **Listings of property for sale and number of sales:** Just as the construction of many new buildings is bad for future real estate price appreciation, increasing numbers of property listings are an indication of potential trouble. A sign of a healthy real estate market is a decreasing and relatively low level of property listings, indicating that the demand from buyers meets or exceeds the supply of property for sale from sellers. When the cost of buying is relatively low compared with the cost of renting, more renters can afford and choose to purchase, thus increasing the number of sales.

✓ **Rental rates:** The trend in rental rates that renters are willing and able to pay over the years is a good indication of the demand for housing. When the demand for housing keeps up with the supply of housing and the local economy continues to grow, rents generally increase. This increase is a positive sign for continued real estate price appreciation. Beware of buying rental property that's subject to rent control; the property's expenses may rise faster than you can raise the rents.

Valuing property and financial projections

Crunching some numbers to figure what revenue and expenses a rental property may have is one of the most important exercises that you can go through when determining a property's worth and making an offer. Here are some key things to do:

✔ **Estimate cash flow.** Cash flow is the difference between the money that a property brings in and what goes out for its expenses.

✔ **Value property.** Estimating a property's cash flow is an important first step in figuring a property's value, but a building's cash flow doesn't provide enough information for you to decide intelligently whether to buy a particular real estate investment. Property valuations are most often done by appraisers, who value property for a living, or real estate agents, who can do an analysis of comparable property sales.

For more details on investing in real estate, see *Real Estate Investing For Dummies,* 2nd Edition (Wiley), which I cowrote with Robert S. Griswold.

Chapter 12

Taking Your Talents to the Small-Business Arena

● ●

In This Chapter

▶ Making the most of your jobs and career

▶ Testing your entrepreneurial mettle

▶ Weighing your small-business investment options

● ●

The American Dream isn't a 9-to-5 job working for someone else, especially a large company, during your entire working career. Many people dream of starting and running their own business. Making plenty of money, being one's own boss, and having flexibility in setting your hours are often part of the dream.

I've known plenty of dreamers over the years, as well as those who achieved their dream. This chapter is designed to help you to invest in yourself by making the most of your working years and figuring out how to pursue entrepreneurial endeavors, if that's what you desire. I also discuss alternative ways to invest in small business that don't involve starting a business from scratch.

Investing in Your Career

Some people aren't going to enjoy — or be successful — as entrepreneurs. The simple truth and reality is that some folks are better off working for someone else. Some people are happy or content as employees. There are plenty of solid companies that need and want good employees, so you should be able to find a desirable job if you have skills, a good work ethic, and the ability to get along with others.

With the relatively weak economy in the late 2000s and early 2010s, some folks continue to have difficulty finding desirable work to fit their skills. The global economy is increasingly competitive, and those whose skills don't measure up will have a harder time finding the best jobs at the best wages.

You can make the most of your income-earning ability and invest in your career in a variety of ways:

- ✔ **Get useful experience.** You probably have in your mind at least a dream job (working for a company or organization). The reality, however, is that you may not have the requisite training and experience to land the dream job right now. So you have to figure out what jobs will allow you to tap your talents and help you gain needed experience to realize your dream.

- ✔ **Read.** One of the reasons you don't need an advanced degree or even a fancy liberal-arts undergraduate college degree to succeed in business is that you can find out a lot on your own. You can gain insight by doing, but you can also gain expertise by reading. A good bookstore or well-stocked library has no entrance requirements, such as a high grade-point average or SAT score. A good book costs a heck of a lot less than taking college or graduate courses!

- ✔ **Continue your education.** If you haven't completed your college or graduate degree and the industry you're in values those who have, consider investing the time and money to finish your education. Speak with others who have taken that path, and see what they have to say. Also, check out the increasing numbers of online courses being offered for free by good schools on sites like www.academicearth.org and www.coursera.org.

- ✔ **Work hard.** Be willing to work extra hours and take on more responsibility. Those who take extra initiative and then deliver really stand out in a company where many people working on a salary have a time-clock, 9-to-5 mentality. Be careful, however, that the extra effort doesn't contribute to workaholism, a dangerous addiction that causes folks to neglect important personal relationships and their own health. Don't bite off more than you can chew; otherwise, your supervisors won't have faith that they can count on you to deliver. Find ways to work smarter, not just longer, hours.

Deciding to Start Your Own Business

Should you start your own business? It's often a tough decision for most people, and it's the first question you should answer before turning your business idea into the reality of your start-up company. In addition to helping you decide whether to start your own business, in this section I discuss a potentially attractive alternative: being an entrepreneur inside an established company.

Weighing your options

Of all your small-business options, starting your own business involves the greatest amount of work. Although you can perform this work on a part-time basis in the beginning, most people end up working in their business full-time.

For most of my working years, I've run my own business, and overall, I really like it. In my experience counseling small-business owners, I've seen many people of varied backgrounds, interests, and skills achieve success and happiness running their own businesses.

Most people perceive starting their own business as the riskiest of all small-business investment options. But if you get into a business that uses your skills and expertise, the risk isn't nearly as great as you may think.

Instead of leaving your job cold turkey and trying to build your business from scratch, you may be able to make progress by moonlighting. Many an entrepreneur has laid a nice foundation for his business over a couple of years by building up his business in this fashion.

You can start many businesses with little money by leveraging your existing skills and expertise. If you have the time to devote to building sweat equity, you can build a valuable company and job. As long as you check out the competition and offer a valued product or service at a reasonable cost, a principal risk with your business is that you won't do a good job of marketing what you have to offer.

Sometimes, entrepreneurial advocates imply that running your own business or starting your own not-for-profit organization is the greatest thing in the world and that all people would be happy owning their own businesses if they just set their minds to it. Starting and running a business aren't for everyone, though. The good news: Other options may offer you the best of both worlds.

Entrepreneuring at a company

Wouldn't it be great if you could have a job that gave you the challenge and upside of running your own business, with the security and support that come with a company environment? This combination does exist — if you can manage an entrepreneurial venture at a company.

If you're able to secure an entrepreneurial position inside a larger company, in addition to gaining significant managerial and operational responsibility, you can negotiate your share of the financial success that you help create. The parent company's senior management wants you to have the incentive that comes from sharing in the financial success of your endeavors. Bonuses, stock options, and the like are often tied to a division's performance.

For more small-business options beyond starting your own business or leading an entrepreneurial effort inside an established company, see "Considering Small-Business Investment Options," later in this chapter.

Turning a Business Idea into Reality

Ideas are a dime a dozen. I'd love to see you turn your best ideas into reality. To make that happen, you should develop a business plan, lay the groundwork financially and emotionally to leave your job, and determine how you're going to finance your new venture. I cover these topics in this section.

Drawing up your business plan

If you're motivated to start your own business, the next step is to prepare a business plan. Your business plan should be a working document or blueprint for the early days, months, and years of your business. It should enable you to plan your goals, obtain loans, and show potential investors what you plan to do with any money they would invest in or loan to your business.

The amount of detail that your plan needs depends on your goals and the specifics of your business. A simple, more short-term-focused plan of 10 pages or less is fine if your goal is a "smaller" small business. However, if your goal is to grow, hire employees, and open multiple locations, your plan generally needs to be more substantial (30 to 50 pages) to address longer-term issues. If you want to solicit outside investors, a longer business plan is a necessity.

As you put together your business plan and evaluate your opportunities and challenges, keep your ears and eyes open. Expect to do research, and speak with other entrepreneurs and people in the industry. Most folks will spend time talking with you as long as they realize that you don't want to compete with their businesses.

What follows are the highlights your business plan should cover:

✓ **The executive summary:** An executive summary is a two- to three-page summary of your entire business plan that you can share with interested investors who don't have the time and desire to wade through a lengthy plan. The executive summary whets the prospective investor's appetite by touching on the highlights of your entire plan.

✓ **Business-concept definition:** What do you want your business to do? What product or service do you want to offer? Your concept doesn't need to be unique to survive in the business world. The existence of plenty of other businesses doing what you want to do validates the potential for your small-business ideas. I'm not suggesting that an innovative idea lacks merit. Indeed, a creative idea gives you the chance to hit it big, and being the first person to successfully develop a new idea can help you achieve big success.

✓ **Your objectives:** Before starting your firm, think about your objectives, or what you're seeking to achieve. Your objectives will likely evolve over time. Most for-profit businesses, not surprisingly, seek to maximize profits. Other common objectives can include working with people you like and respect, educating others, and improving an industry or setting a higher standard. You can't accomplish these loftier objectives without profits, of course, and doing these things isn't inconsistent with generating greater profits.

✔ **Understanding of the marketplace:** The single most important area to understand is the marketplace in which your business competes. To be successful, your business must not only produce a good product or service, but also reach customers and persuade them to buy your product at a price at which you can make a profit. So you must understand your desired customers and their needs. Discern what the competition has to offer, as well as its strengths and weaknesses. You also need to understand government regulations that affect the type of business that you're considering.

✔ **Plans to deliver your service or product:** How are you going to provide your product or service to your customers? If you want to manufacture a product, you definitely need to scope out the process that you're going to use. Otherwise, you have no idea how much time the manufacturing process may take or what the process may cost. As your business grows and you hire employees to provide services or create your products, the more you document what you do, and the better your employees can replicate your good work.

✔ **Plans to market your service or product:** How much will you charge for your services and products? How will you position your products and services compared with the competition? Where will you sell your product or service? Finding and retaining customers is vital to any business owner who wants her company to grow and be profitable. One simple, inexpensive way to stay in touch with customers you've dealt with or others who have made inquiries and expressed interest in your company's offerings is via a mailing list. Software and websites (such as Constant Contact) give you fast, efficient ways to keep customer mailing lists up to date and print mailing labels if desired.

✔ **Plans to organize and staff your business:** Many small businesses are one-person operations — so much the better for you if that's what you desire, because you'll have none of the headaches of hiring, payroll, and so on. But if you hope to grow your business and would rather manage the work being done instead of doing all of it yourself, you'll eventually want to hire people. Give some thought now to the skills and functional areas of expertise that future hires will need. If you want to raise money, the employment section of your business plan is essential to show your investors that you're planning long-term. Also consider what legal form of organization — sole proprietorship, partnership, S corporation, limited liability company, and so on — your business will adopt. This decision affects how the business is taxed and what its liabilities are in the event of a lawsuit, among other important issues.

✔ **Financial projections:** An idea may become a business failure if you neglect to consider, or are unrealistic about, the financial side of the business that you want to start. Financial projections are mandatory, and knowledgeable investors will scrutinize them if you seek outside money. Before the revenue begins to flow in, you incur expenditures as you develop and market your products and services. Therefore, you need to understand what you must spend money on and the approximate timing of the needed purchases. Preparing an estimated income statement that summarizes your expected revenue and expenses is a challenging and important part of your business plan.

A balance sheet details a company's assets and liabilities. A detailed balance sheet isn't as important as tracking your available cash, which will likely be under pressure in the early years of a business because expenses can continue to exceed revenue for quite some time. A complete balance sheet is useful for a business that owns significant equipment, furniture, inventory, and so on.

After you research and evaluate the needs of your prospective business, at some point you need to decide whether to actually start your business. If you really want to, you can conduct and analyze market research and crunch numbers until the cows come home. Even if you're a linear, logical, analytic, quantitative kind of person, you ultimately need to make a gut-level decision: Do you jump in the water and start swimming, or do you stay on the sidelines and remain a spectator? In my opinion, watching isn't nearly as fun as doing. If you feel ready but have some trepidation, that's normal.

Mind you, I'm not trying to present a rosy view of entrepreneurship. Plenty of small businesses fail, and plenty of small-business owners end up losing rather than making money.

Plotting to leave your job

You may never discover that you have the talent to run your own business, and perhaps have a good idea to boot, unless you prepare yourself financially and psychologically to leave your job. Financial and emotional issues cause many aspiring entrepreneurs to remain chained to their employers and cause those who do break free to soon return to their bondage.

On the financial side, plan for a reduction in the income that you bring home from work, at least in the early years of your business. Do all you can to reduce your expenses to a level that fits the entrepreneurial life that you want to lead. (My book *Personal Finance For Dummies* [Wiley] can help you.)

In addition to reducing your spending before and during the period that you start your business, figure out how to manage the income side of your personal finances. One way to pursue your entrepreneurial dreams is to continue working part-time in a regular job while you work part-time at your own business. If you have a job that allows you to work part-time, seize the opportunity. Just be sure that the outside work you're doing doesn't conflict with your regular job.

Another option is to completely leave your job but line up work that provides a decent income for a portion of your weekly work hours. Consulting for your old employer is a time-tested first "entrepreneurial" option with low risk.

For many people, walking away from their employer's benefits (including insurance, retirement funds, and paid time off) is both financially and emotionally challenging. Benefits are valuable, but you may be surprised by how efficiently you can replicate them in your own business:

> ✔ **Health insurance:** Unless you have a preexisting medical condition, getting health insurance as an individual isn't difficult. If you have such a condition, many states have high-risk pools that offer coverage options, and effective in 2014, group health plans may no longer impose such restrictions. The first option to explore is whether your existing coverage through your employer's group plan can be converted to individual coverage (through COBRA). Also, get proposals for individual coverage from major health plans in your area. Take a high deductible, if available, to keep costs down. Having a high-deductible health

plan, which is defined as an individual plan with a deductible of at least $1,200 or a family plan with a minimum $2,400 deductible for tax year 2012 (this amount increases over time with inflation), qualifies you to contribute money to a health savings account (HSA). Contributions to an HSA reduce your current year's taxable income, and the money compounds without taxation over time. Withdrawals aren't taxed so long as you use the money for qualified health-care expenses, which are broadly defined.

✔ **Long-term disability insurance:** Your greatest asset probably is your ability to earn money. Long-term disability (LTD) insurance protects your work income in the event of a disability. Before you leave your job, secure an individual LTD policy. After you leave your job and are no longer earning steady income, you won't qualify for a policy. Check with any professional associations that you belong to or could join to see whether they offer LTD plans. Association plans are sometimes less expensive because of the group's purchasing power.

✔ **Life insurance:** If you have dependents who count on your income, you need life insurance. You can generally purchase a life insurance policy on your own for less money than additional coverage through your employer would cost.

✔ **Retirement savings plans:** If your employer offers retirement savings programs, such as a 401(k) plan or a pension plan, don't despair about not having these in the future. One of the best benefits of self-employment is the availability of SEP-IRAs and Keoghs, which allow you to sock away up to 20 percent of your net income on a tax-deductible basis. With employees, the decision is a bit more complicated but often still a great idea.

Financing your business

While creating your business plan (discussed earlier in the chapter), you should estimate your business's start-up and development costs. Luckily, you can start many worthwhile small businesses with little capital, but you will need capital — and for some businesses, significant amounts.

Here are proven, time-tested methods of financing your business:

✔ **Bootstrapping:** *Bootstrapping* simply means that a business lives within its own means and without external support. This funding strategy generally forces a business to be more resourceful and less wasteful. Bootstrapping is also a great training mechanism for producing cost-effective products and services. It offers you the advantage of getting into business with little capital.

Misconceptions abound about how much money a company needs to achieve its goals and sources of funding. The vast majority of small businesses obtain their initial capital from personal savings, relatives, and friends rather than from outside sources, such as banks and venture capital firms. A Harvard Business School study of the *Inc.* 500 (fast-growing private companies) found that more than 80 percent of the successful companies started with funds from the founder's personal savings. The median start-up capital was a modest $10,000, and these are successful, fast-growing companies! Slower-growing companies tend to require even less capital.

Eventually, a successful, growing company may want outside financing to expand faster. Raising money from investors or lenders is much easier after you demonstrate that you know what you're doing and that a market exists for your product or service.

✔ **Taking out business loans:** If you're starting a new business or have been in business for just a few years, borrowing, particularly from banks, may be difficult. Borrowing money is easier when you don't really need to do so. No one knows this fact better than small-business owners. To borrow money from a bank, you generally need a business plan, three years of financial statements and tax returns for the business and its owner, and projections for the business. Seek out banks that are committed to and understand the small-business marketplace.

The U.S. Small Business Administration (SBA) offers workshops and counseling services for small-business owners. Its SCORE (Service Corps of Retired Executives) consulting services (www.score.org; 800-634-0245) provide free advice and critiques of business plans, as well as advice on raising money for your business. For more information on the SBA's services and how to contact a local office, call 800-827-5722, or visit its website at www.sba.gov.

If you don't have luck with banks or the SBA, credit unions can be a source of financial help. They're often more willing to make personal loans to individuals.

✔ **Borrowing from relatives and friends:** Because they know you and (ideally) like and trust you, your family members and friends may seem like good sources of investment money for your small business. They also likely have the added advantage of offering you better terms than a banker, wealthy investor, or a venture capitalist. Be sure to prepare and sign a letter of agreement that spells out the terms of the investment or loan, and that states that you had a candid discussion with all involved as to the risks and downside if things don't work out the way you hope.

✔ **Tapping investors for an equity investment:** Beyond family members and friends, wealthy individuals are your next best source of capital if you want an equity investor. An *angel investor* is a wealthy individual who invests in small companies and has a track record of success in funding somewhat-similar businesses. Angels bring things to the table besides money, such as strategic advice and helpful business contacts.

Finding folks who may be interested in investing requires persistence and creativity. Try consulting tax advisors and attorneys you know who may have contacts, and network with successful entrepreneurs in similar fields. Also consider customers or suppliers who like your business and believe in its potential.

Considering Small-Business Investment Options

Only your imagination limits the ways you can make money with small businesses. Choosing the option that best meets your needs isn't unlike choosing other investments, such as in real estate or in the financial markets. In this section, I discuss the major ways you can invest in small business, including what's attractive and not so attractive about each option.

Buying an existing business

If you don't have a specific idea for a business that you want to start, but you have business management skills and an ability to improve existing businesses, consider buying an established business.

Although you don't have to go through the riskier start-up period if you take this route, you'll likely need more capital to buy a going enterprise. You also need to be able to deal with potentially sticky personnel and management issues. The history of the organization and the way things work predate your ownership of the business. If you don't like making hard decisions, firing people who don't fit with your plans, and coercing people to change the way they did things before you arrived on the scene, buying an existing business likely isn't for you. Also realize that some of the good employees may be loyal to the old owner and his style of running the business, so they may split when you arrive.

Some people perceive that buying an existing business is safer than starting a new one, but buying someone else's business can actually be riskier. You have to put out far more money up front, in the form of a down payment, to buy a business. And if you don't have the ability to run the business, and it does poorly, you may lose much more financially. Another risk is that the business may be for sale for a reason. Perhaps it's not very profitable, it's in decline, or it's generally a pain in the posterior to operate.

Good businesses that are for sale don't come cheaply. If the business is a success, the current owner has removed the start-up risk from the business, so the price of the business should include a premium to reflect this lack of risk. If you have the capital to buy an established business and the skills to run it, consider going this route.

Investing in someone else's business

If you like the idea of profiting from successful small businesses but don't want the day-to-day responsibility of managing the enterprise, you may want to invest in someone else's small business. Although this route may seem easier, fewer people are actually cut out to be investors in other people's businesses.

Consider investing in someone else's business if the following points describe you:

- ✔ **You have sufficient assets:** You need enough assets so that what you invest in small, privately held companies is a small portion (20 percent or less) of your total financial assets.

- ✔ **You can afford to lose what you invest:** Unlike with investing in a diversified stock fund, you may lose all your investment when you invest in a small, privately held company.

- ✔ **You're astute at evaluating financial statements and business strategies:** Investing in a small, privately held company has much in common with investing in a publicly traded firm. A main difference is that private firms aren't required to produce comprehensive, audited financial statements that adhere to certain accounting principles, the way that public companies are. Thus, you have a greater risk of not receiving sufficient or accurate information when you evaluate a small private firm. (There are also liquidity differences, in that with a small, private company, you may not be able to sell out when you want and at a fair current price.)

Putting money into your own business (or someone else's) can be a high-risk but potentially high-return investment. The best options are those that you understand well. If you hear about a great business idea or company from someone you know and trust, do your research, and use your best judgment. That company or idea may be a terrific investment.

Before investing, read and review the business plan. Thoroughly check out the people who are running the business. Talk to others who don't have a stake in the investment; you can benefit from their comments and concerns. Remember, though, that many a wise person has rained on the parade of what turned out to be a terrific business idea.

Chapter 13

Exploring Other Investment Vehicles

● ●

In This Chapter

▶ Gold and other commodities

▶ Collectibles

▶ Annuities and insurance

● ●

*I*n the earlier chapters of this book, I present and discuss a pretty wide range of investments that are time-tested. You've probably already heard of and been pitched "other investments." The vast majority of these alternative investments are flawed due to high fees, lousy performance, or worse.

In this chapter, I discuss the most common of these alternative investments: gold and other commodities, collectibles, and annuities and cash-value life insurance. In each case, I explain each investment's redeeming qualities as well as its flaws.

Considering Gold and Other Precious Metals

Of all the commodities, gold and silver have gotten the most attention over time, especially in recent decades. Gold and silver are also known as *precious metals.*

Gold and silver have served as mediums of exchange or currency over thousands of years because they have tangible value and can't be debased the way that paper currencies can (by printing more money). These precious metals are used in jewelry and manufacturing.

As investments, gold and silver perform well during bouts of inflation, especially when the inflation is unexpected. During the 1970s, for example, when inflation zoomed into the double-digit range in the United States and stocks and bonds went into the tank, gold and silver prices skyrocketed more than 500 percent.

Precious-metals prices have zoomed upward again since 2000. From less than $300 per ounce, gold hit more than $1,900 per ounce in the early 2010s, as some feared the return of inflation due to excessive government debt, government stimulus spending, and expansion of the printed money supply. During this period, silver jumped from just over $4 per ounce to a high of $45 per ounce.

Although precious metals may shine for a decade, over the long, long term, they're lousy investments. They don't pay any dividends, and their price increases may at best just keep up with, but not ahead of, increases in the cost of living. Consider the fact that even with gold breaching $1,900 per ounce in 2011, it was still below the inflation-adjusted levels it reached more than 30 years ago. To reach those levels, gold would have to rise to more than $2,300 an ounce!

Although investing in precious metals is better than keeping cash in a piggy bank or stuffing it in a mattress, the long-term investment returns aren't nearly as good as those of bonds, stocks, and real estate. One way to earn better long-term returns is to invest in a fund containing the stocks of gold and precious-metals companies.

One such fund to consider is the Vanguard Precious Metals and Mining fund (trading symbol VGPMX). This presents an interesting alternative to investing directly in precious metals. VGPMX invests in companies that benefit from increased demand for physical assets such as gold, other precious metals, and minerals.

Gold and collectibles don't get favorable capital gains tax treatment

While gold and other precious metals have increased in value over the years, they've produced returns significantly below stocks and even bonds. And unbeknownst to most investors, the profits on precious metals aren't eligible for the low 15-percent tax rate cap on long-term capital gains (for investments held more than one year). Collectibles, which includes precious metals, are taxed at nearly double that rate — 28 percent — which further reduces the sub-par return on gold and other precious metals.

Historically, investors haven't been allowed to own gold and other collectibles in retirement accounts. However, investors in precious metals were happy to hear that in 2007, the IRS ruled that investors could own precious metal ETFs in retirement accounts since ETFs are shares of ownership and not a direct stake in a precious metal.

"This ruling hinges on the ETF being formed as a trust. The shareholders of the ETF do not have claims on the bullion owned by the fund and can't ask for distributions of the metal," says Bob Carlson, who publishes the *Retirement Watch* newsletter.

However, a more recent IRS ruling contained bad tax news for investors holding gold and other precious ETFs in taxable (nonretirement) accounts: "... If the investor sells shares in the ETF, the investor is treated as selling his or her share of the metal backing the shares. When the investor owned the shares for more than one year, the gains are taxed at the 28 percent rate instead of the 15 percent rate," says Carlson.

Of course, if you own the ETF in a retirement account, you lose all possible preferential capital gains tax treatment. Upon withdrawal from a retirement account, all profits are taxed as ordinary income.

Since the fund's inception in 1984, it has returned 6.6 percent per year, which is about double the returns posted by gold. Going forward, also consider the fact that gold pays no dividends. The Vanguard fund sports a current dividend yield of more than 2 percent.

 Be aware that VGPMX is quite volatile. That fact is borne out by the wide swings in the fund's annual performance in absolute terms as well as within its peer group.

Contemplating Collectibles

The term *collectibles* is a catch-all category for antiques, art, autographs of famous folks, baseball cards, clocks, coins, comic books, diamonds, dolls, gems, photographs, rare books, rugs, stamps, vintage wine, writing utensils, and a whole host of other items. In this section, I discuss the appeal and reality of investing in collectibles.

Understanding the allure of collectibles

The best returns that collectibles investors reap come from the ability to identify, years in advance, items that will become popular. Do you think you can do that? You may be the smartest person in the world, but you should know that most dealers can't tell what's going to rocket to popularity in the coming decades.

Dealers make their profits the same way other retailers do — from the spread or markup on the merchandise that they sell. The public and collectors have fickle, quirky tastes that no one can predict. Who knew in advance that Beanie Babies, Furbies, Pet Rocks, and Cabbage Patch Kids were going to be such hits?

You can find out enough about a specific type of collectible to become a better investor than the average person, but you have to be among the best such collectors to have a shot at earning decent returns. To get to this level of expertise, you need to invest hundreds, if not thousands, of hours reading, researching, and educating yourself about your specific type of collectible.

Don't get me wrong: There's nothing wrong with spending money on collectibles. Just don't fool yourself into thinking that they're investments (more on their actual returns in the next section). You can sink lots of your money into these non-income-producing, poor-return "investments." At their best as investments, collectibles give the wealthy a way to buy quality stuff that doesn't depreciate.

Seeing the realities of collectibles and their returns

Although connoisseurs of fine art, antiques, and vintage wine wouldn't like the comparison of their pastime with buying old playing cards, collectibles generally are objects with little intrinsic value. Wine is just a bunch of old, mushed-up grapes. A painting is simply a canvas and some paint that at retail would set you back a few bucks. Stamps are small pieces of paper, usually less than an inch square. What about baseball cards? Heck, my childhood friends and I used to stick them between our bike spokes (the crummiest players' cards, of course)!

I'm not trying to diminish contributions that artists and others make to the world's culture. And I know that some people place a high value on some of these collectibles. But true investments that can make your money grow — such as stocks, real estate, or a small business — are assets that can produce income and profits.

Collectibles have little intrinsic value and, thus, are fully exposed to the whims and speculations of buyers and sellers. As history has shown, of course, and as I discuss elsewhere in the book, the prices of particular stocks, real estate, and businesses can be subject to the whims and speculations of buyers and sellers, too, especially in the short term. Over the long term, however, securities' market prices return to reality and sensible valuations. Also, a real investment can provide a return to you even if no one ever buys it from you.

Here are some other major problems with collectibles:

- ✔ **Large markup costs:** The spread between the price that a dealer pays for an object and the price for which he sells the same object is often around 100 percent. Sometimes, the difference is even greater, particularly if a dealer is the second or third middleman in the chain of purchase. So at minimum, your purchase typically must double in value just to get you back to even, and a value may not double for 10 to 20 years or more!

✔ **Substantial other costs:** If the markups aren't bad enough, some collectibles incur all sorts of other costs. If you buy more-expensive pieces, for example, you may need to have them appraised. You may have to pay storage and insurance costs as well. And unlike the case with markup, you pay some of these fees year after year of ownership.

✔ **Costly mistakes of nonexpert buyers:** Sometimes, you may overpay even more for a collectible because you didn't realize some imperfection or inferiority of the item. Worse, you may buy a forgery. Even reputable dealers have been duped by forgeries. Also, you may make storage mistakes that cause your collectible to deteriorate over time. Damage from sunlight, humidity, temperatures that are too high or too low, and a whole host of vagaries can ruin the quality of your collectible. Insurance doesn't cover this type of damage or negligence on your part.

✔ **Terrible returns:** Even if you ignore the substantial costs of buying, holding, and selling, the average returns that investors earn from collectibles rarely keep ahead of inflation, and they're generally inferior to returns from stocks, real estate, and small-business investing.

Objective return data on collectibles is hard to come by. Never, ever trust so-called "data" that dealers or the many collectibles trade publications provide.

Considering advice on buying collectibles

If you want to buy collectibles and can afford to do so, you have my blessing. Here are some tips to keep in mind to make the most of your efforts:

✔ **Do your homework.** Use a comprehensive resource to research, buy, sell, maintain, and improve your collectible, such as the books by Ralph and Terry Kovel or their website at www.kovels.com.

✔ **Collect for your love of the collectible, your desire to enjoy it, or your interest in finding out about or mastering a subject.** In other words, don't collect these items because you expect high investment returns, because you probably won't get them.

✓ **When you know what you want, buy direct, and eliminate the middleman where possible.** In some cases, you may be able to buy directly from the artist.

✓ **Check collectibles that are comparable to the one you have your eye on, shop around, and don't be afraid to negotiate.** An effective way to negotiate after you decide what you like is to make your offer to the dealer or artist by phone. Because the seller isn't standing right next to you, you don't feel pressure to decide immediately.

✓ **Get a buy-back guarantee.** Ask the dealer (who thinks that the item is such a great investment) for a written guarantee to buy the item back from you within five years, if you opt to sell it, for at least the same price you paid for it.

✓ **Keep quality items that you and your family have purchased, and hope that someday they'll be worth something.** Keeping these quality items is the simplest way to break into the collectibles business. The complete sets of baseball cards I gathered as a youngster are now (30-plus years later) worth hundreds of dollars, and one is worth $1,000!

Understanding Annuities and Cash-Value Life Insurance

Odds are that if you're looking to make investments, you'll be pitched various types of investment vehicles by folks who are licensed to sell insurance products. In this section, I discuss two of the most common vehicles: annuities and cash-value life insurance.

Availing yourself of annuities

Annuities are contracts that insurance companies back. If you, the annuity holder (investor), should die during the so-called accumulation phase (before receiving payments from the annuity), your designated beneficiary is guaranteed reimbursement of the amount of your original investment.

Annuities, like Individual Retirement Accounts (IRAs), allow your capital to grow and compound tax-deferred. You defer taxes until you withdraw the money. Unlike with an IRA, which has an annual contribution limit of $5,000, you can deposit as much as you want into an annuity in any year — even millions of dollars, if you've got them! As with a Roth IRA, however, you get no up-front tax deduction for your contributions.

The problem with annuities is that insurance agents try to sell them to many folks who won't benefit from them — and the vast majority of folks won't be in a position to benefit from them.

If you've contributed all you're allowed to contribute to your IRA and your employer's retirement accounts, and you still want to put more money into retirement accounts, you might consider annuities.

Don't consider contributing to an annuity until you've fully exhausted your other retirement account investing options. The reason: Annuity contributions aren't tax-deductible, and annuities carry higher annual operating fees to pay for the small amount of insurance that comes with them. Because of their higher annual expenses, annuities generally make sense only if you have 15 or more years to wait until you need the money.

Considering cash-value life insurance

If you have dependents, you may need life insurance. The key question to ask yourself and your family is how they would fare if you died and they no longer had your employment income. You need life insurance if your family is dependent on your income from work and would be unable to maintain its current standard of living with your passing.

Term life insurance is pure insurance protection and the best choice for the vast majority of people. The other major type of life insurance is *cash-value coverage,* which includes a life insurance death benefit (as does a term policy), as well as a savings and investment feature.

You generally can't combine insurance with investing when you buy an auto, disability, or homeowner's policy, so why can you with life insurance? You can thanks to an exemption in the tax code.

Insurance companies and agents who sell their products and earn commissions favor cash-value life insurance. The reasons are pretty simple: Cash-value life insurance costs much more and provides heftier profits for insurance companies and commissions to the agents who sell it.

You should consider getting cash-value life insurance only if your net worth is high enough that you anticipate having an estate-planning "problem." When you buy a cash-value policy and place it in an irrevocable life insurance trust, the death benefits can pass to your heirs free of federal estate taxes.

Under current tax law, you can leave up to $5.12 million free of federal estate taxes to your heirs. (These laws may change in 2013 with changes in Washington.) If you're married, you can pass on double these amounts through the use of a bypass trust. So, most people don't have an estate-planning situation that warrants cash-value life insurance.

Part V
The Part of Tens

The 5th Wave   By Rich Tennant

In this part...

I present some quick-reference chapters that contain ten important points each. The topics include ten things to know about investment information sources and the ten investment concepts that contribute greatly to investing success.

Chapter 14

Ten Things to Know About Investing Resources

*E*verywhere you look or listen, you'll find plenty — and I mean plenty — of investing opinions and advice. Some of it may be great information but not a good fit for you. Much of it is mediocre or downright awful and misleading.

In this chapter, I highlight ten important things you should know and do to evaluate investing resources and get the right information for you.

Get Educated to Discern the Best from the Rest

With the tremendous increase in the coverage of investing, more and more journalists are writing about increasingly technical issues — often in areas in which they have no expertise. (This type of reporting is true in traditional print publications but especially so online.) Some writers provide good information and advice. Unfortunately, many others dish out bad or mediocre advice.

How can you know what information is good and whom you can trust? Although I suggest my favorite resources later in this chapter, I know that you'll encounter many investment resources, and you need to know how to tell the best from the rest. The answer rests in educating yourself. The more knowledgeable you are about sound and flawed investment strategies, the better able you are to tell good from not-so-good investment resources.

Beware "Free"

Too many folks get suckered into supposedly free resources when looking for investing information and advice. The Internet is filled with tons of "free" investing sites, and if you turn on your television or radio, you come across mountains of "free" stuff. Someone is paying for all this "free" content, of course, and it's all available for some reason.

Most of the free Internet sites are run by investment companies or someone else (such as small-time money managers) with something to sell. What these sites give away is nothing but subtle and not-so-subtle advertising for whatever products and services they sell. Many investing books also contain thinly veiled advertisements. Some so-called authors choose to write books that are the equivalent of infomercials for something else — such as high-priced seminars — that they really want to sell you. Such writers aren't interested in educating and helping you as much as they're seeking to sell you something else. So, for example, an author may write about how complicated the investing markets are, saying that investing is too complicated to do on your own and that you really need a personal investment manager like the author.

Understand the Influence of Advertising

Whether on the Internet, on television, in print, or on the radio, advertising often compromises the quality of the investment advice it accompanies. I won't say that you can't find some useful investment resources in media with lots of advertising. These resources, however, are exceptions to the rule that sources with lots of advertising contain little valuable information and advice.

Many organizations, such as newspaper and magazine publishing companies and radio and television stations that accept ads, say that their ad departments are separate from their editorial departments. The truth, however, is that in most of these organizations, advertisers wield influence over the content. At minimum, the editorial environments at these organizations must be perceived as being conducive to the sale of the advertisers' products.

The influence of advertisers prevents readers, viewers, and listeners from getting the truth and best advice. Specifically, some media organizations and publishers simply won't make derogatory comments about advertisers, and sometimes, they highlight and praise investment companies that are big advertisers.

Value Quality over Quantity

Talk about information overload! Blogs on the topic of investing continue to multiply. You can't peruse a newspaper or magazine or turn on the television or radio without bumping into articles, stories, segments, and entire programs devoted to investment issues.

The explosion of the Internet has introduced a whole new medium. Now, at a relatively low cost, anyone can publish content online. The number of television channels has mushroomed as a result of cable television. Flip through your cable channels at any hour of the day, and you see infomercials that promise to make you a real estate tycoon or stock market millionaire in your spare time. These newer communications options are primarily structured around selling advertising rather than offering quality content. The accessibility of these communications media allows just about anyone with an animated personality or access to a computer to appear to be an expert. Much of the advice out there can easily steer you in the wrong direction.

Because investment information and advice is so widespread and constantly growing, knowing how to sift through it is just as important as hearing what the best resources are today. When chosen wisely, the best investing resources can further your investment knowledge and enable you to make better decisions. Quality is more important that quantity. Later in this chapter, I name the best investment resources that I'm familiar with.

Know How to Check Out a Resource

The best thing to do when you encounter a financial magazine, website, newspaper, or other resource for the first time is scrutinize it.

All things being equal, you have a greater chance of finding quality content when subscriber fees account for the bulk of a company's revenue and advertising accounts for little or none of the revenue. This generalization, of course, is just that: a generalization. Some publications that derive a reasonable portion of their revenue from advertising have some good columns and content. Conversely, some relatively ad-free sources aren't very good.

Deciphering a writer's philosophy and agenda is important in determining whether he provides quality information. Readers of my books, for example, can clearly understand my philosophies about investing. I advocate buying and holding, not trading and gambling. I explain how to build wealth through proven vehicles, including stocks, real estate, and small-business ownership.

Unfortunately, many publications and programs don't make it as easy for you to see or hear their operating beliefs. You have to do some homework. With a radio program, for example, you probably have to listen to at least portions of several shows to get a sense of the host's investment philosophies.

Examine the backgrounds, including professional work experience and education credentials, of a resource's writers, hosts, or anchors. If such information isn't given or easily found, consider this secrecy to be a red flag. People who have something to hide or who lack solid credentials usually don't promote their backgrounds. Also, don't blindly accept presented qualifications as being honest or truthful.

Red flags include publications and programs that make investing sound overly complicated and that imply — or say outright — that you won't succeed or do as well if you don't hire a financial advisor or follow your investments like a hawk.

Beware Hype and Exaggeration

There's an old news-media expression, "If it bleeds, it leads." Translated, this means that jarring, violent, or blood-and-gore stories attract attention.

Too often, this is the case in financial reporting too. If the stock market drops quickly or there's a disappointing economic report, you're sure to hear about it over and over again.

I'm not suggesting that only good news be reported. But frequently, negative events are blown out of proportion and hyped to garner more attention. Don't get carried away by the hype.

Don't Assume Quoted Experts Know Their Stuff

Historically, one way that investment journalists have attempted to overcome technical gaps in their knowledge has been to interview and quote experts in the field. Although these quotes may add to the accuracy and quality of a story, journalists who aren't experts themselves often have difficulty telling qualified experts from hacks.

One common example of this phenomenon is that many investment writers quote unproven advice from investment-newsletter writers. As I discuss later in this chapter, the predictive advice of many newsletter writers is often poor, causing investors to earn lower returns and miss investment gains due to frequent trading. Journalists who simply parrot this type of information and provide an endorsement that unqualified sources are "experts" do readers an immense disservice.

Investigate Gurus' Claims

The tremendous growth in the number of people talking and writing about investing on websites, on cable television, and on radio means that more pundits are making claims about the value of their predictions. Unfortunately, many publications and media outlets that interview and give air time to these pundits fail to independently investigate most such claims.

You don't need predictions and soothsayers to make sound investing choices. If you choose to follow this "expert" advice and you're lucky, little harm will be done. But more often than not, you can lose lots of money by following a pundit's predictions.

Never accept a guru's performance claims as valid. These claims should always be verified through an independent source. Visit the "Guru Watch" section of my website, www. erictyson.com, for analysis of many of the popular gurus in the media today.

Don't Believe Investment-Newsletter Claims

Especially in the investment-newsletter business, you'll see and hear lots of extraordinary performance claims. Private money managers, who aren't subject to the same scrutiny and auditing requirements as fund managers, can do the same.

Be especially wary of any newsletters making claims of high returns. According to the *Hulbert Financial Digest,* the worst investment newsletters have underperformed the market averages by dozens of percentage points; some would even have caused you to lose money during decades when the financial markets performed extraordinarily well (like the 1980s and 1990s).

Also be aware that plenty of gurus and newsletters will tout many strategies, investments, and funds, and then continue to hype only the one that happens to do well. The strategy or back-tested model may in fact have a good track record over a given period, but it may be cherry-picked and unlikely to succeed in the future.

Don't believe a track record unless a reputable accounting firm with experience doing such audits has audited it. Stay far away from publications that purport to be able to tell what's going to happen next. No one has a crystal ball.

Check Out and Keep Up with My Favorite Resources

I've come across a lot of resources over the years. Some have stood the test of time and offer worthwhile perspectives and insights. Here are some of the best for you to consider:

- ✔ www.corporateinformation.com: If you want to pick your own stocks, this site has a treasure trove of information, but subscription fees aren't cheap.

- ✔ www.morningstar.com: The premium content here, which is more moderately priced, covers all types of funds and most stocks.

- ✔ *A Random Walk Down Wall Street: The Time-Tested Strategy for Successful Investing,* by Burton G. Malkiel (W.W. Norton): I first read this classic in a college economics course, and this book has gotten better over the years, with its new editions.

- ✔ www.sec.gov: The U.S. Securities and Exchange Commission provides free access to the regulatory-required filings of investment funds and public companies.

- ✔ www.stlouisfed.org (St. Louis Federal Reserve): This site has lots of interesting economic research and tons of historic economic data.

- ✔ *Stocks for the Long Run: The Definitive Guide to Financial Market Returns & Long Term Investment Strategies,* by Jeremy J. Siegel (McGraw Hill): This terrific book details investing in stocks around the globe over the long run.

- ✔ www.valueline.com: Value Line has generations of experience providing concise summaries for the stocks of public companies.

- ✔ www.vanguard.com: The leading no-load mutual fund company, Vanguard has plenty of user-friendly and readable information on its website.

- ✔ www.erictyson.com: I regularly digest the best financial information and advice and then post the latest on my website. Some content is free, and premium content is available at a relatively low cost.

Chapter 15

Ten Essential Tips for Investing Success

*I*nvesting appears to be complicated and complex. But if you can take some relatively simple concepts to heart and be sure that you adhere to them, you can greatly increase your success.

In this chapter, I present my ten favorite, time-tested principles of investing success. Following these principles will pay you big dividends (and capital gains) for many years to come.

Regularly Save and Invest 5 Percent to 10 Percent of Your Income

Unless you enjoy a large inheritance, you should consistently save 5 percent to 10 percent of the money you're earning. When should you start doing this? I say, as soon as you begin earning money on a regular basis.

Preferably, invest through a retirement savings account to reduce your taxes and ensure your future financial independence. You can reduce both your current federal and state income tax bills (on the contributions) as well as these ongoing bills (on the investment earnings).

The exact amount you should be saving is driven by your goals and by your current financial assets and liabilities. Take the time to crunch some numbers to determine how much you should be saving monthly.

Understand and Use Your Employee Benefits

The larger the employer, the more likely it is to offer avenues for you to invest conveniently through payroll deduction, and with possible tax benefits and discounts. Some companies enable you to buy company stock at a reduced price.

Often, the most valuable benefit you have is a retirement savings plan, such as a 401(k) plan that enables you to make contributions and save on your current income taxation. Also, after the money is in the account, it can compound and grow over the years and decades without taxation.

If you're self-employed, be sure to establish and use a retirement plan (see Chapter 2). Also take time to learn about the best investment options available to you — and use them.

Thoroughly Research Before You Invest

The allure of large expected returns too often is the enticement that gets novices hooked on a particular investment. That's a whole lot more appealing than researching an investment. But research you must if you want to make an informed decision.

Be sure that you understand what you're investing in. Don't purchase any financial product that you don't understand. Ask questions, and compare what you're being offered with the best sources I recommend. Beware of purchasing an investment on the basis of an advertisement or a salesperson's solicitation.

Shun Investments with High Commissions and Expenses

The cost of the investments that you buy is an important variable you can control. All fees must be disclosed in a prospectus, which you should always review before making any investment.

 Companies that sell their investment products through aggressive sales techniques generally have the worst financial products and the highest fees and commissions.

Invest the Majority of Your Long-Term Money in Ownership Investments

When you're young, you have plenty of time to let your investments compound and grow. Likewise, you have time to recover from setbacks.

So with your long-term money, focus on investments that have appreciation potential, such as stocks, real estate, and your own business. When you invest in bonds or bank accounts, you're simply lending your money to others and will earn a return that probably won't keep you ahead of inflation and taxes.

Avoid Making Emotionally Based Financial Decisions

Successful investors keep their composure when the going gets tough. You need the ability and wisdom to look beyond the current environment, understanding that it will change in the months and years ahead.

You don't want to panic and sell your stock holdings after a major market correction, for example. In fact, you should consider such an event to be a buying opportunity for stocks. Be especially careful about making important financial decisions after a major life change, such as marriage, the birth of a child, a divorce, job loss, or a death in your family.

Make Investing Decisions Based on Your Plans and Needs

Your investment decisions should come out of your planning and your overall needs, goals, and desires. This requires looking at your overall financial situation first and then coming up with a comprehensive plan.

Don't be swayed and influenced by the predictive advice offered by various investment pundits or the latest news headlines and concerns. Trust that you know yourself and your financial situation better than anyone else does.

Tap Information Sources with High Quality Standards

You need to pare down the sources you use to keep up with investing news and the financial markets. Give priority to those that aren't afraid to take a stand and recommend what's in your best interests.

Stay away from outlets that cater to advertisers or are driven by an ideological agenda. MSNBC, for example, can't be an objective source of business and economic news because the network's far-left political ideology colors its reporting. On the other side, I haven't found the far-right Glenn Beck to be a useful source of good business and economic information either.

Trust Yourself First

Look in the mirror. You'll see the best financial person that you can hire and trust. What may be missing is enough education and confidence to make more decisions, which this book can assist you with doing.

If you need help making a major decision, hire conflict-free advisors who charge a fee for their time. Work in partnership with advisors. Never turn over or abdicate control.

Invest in Yourself and Others

Don't get so wrapped up in making, saving, and investing money that you lose sight of what matters most to you. Invest in your education, your health, and your relationships with family members and friends.

Having a lot of money isn't worth much if you don't have your health and people with whom to share your life. Give your time and money to causes that better our society and our world.

Index